D1501721

MAO ZEDONG
and the
CHINESE REVOLUTION

MAO ZEDONG
and the
CHINESE REVOLUTION

Corinne J. Naden

MORGAN
REYNOLDS
PUBLISHING

Greensboro, North Carolina

WORLD LEADERS

GEORGE C. MARSHALL
ADOLF HITLER
WOODROW WILSON
VACLAV HAVEL
GENGHIS KHAN
JOSEPH STALIN
CHE GUEVARA
FIDEL CASTRO
HUGO CHAVEZ
MAO ZEDONG

MAO ZEDONG AND THE CHINESE REVOLUTION
Copyright © 2009 By Corinne J. Naden

Library of Congress Cataloging-in-Publication Data

Naden, Corinne J.
   Mao Zedong and the Chinese Revolution / by Corinne J. Naden.
      p. cm.
   Includes bibliographical references and index.
   ISBN-13: 978-1-59935-100-1
   ISBN-10: 1-59935-100-5
   1. Mao, Zedong, 1893-1976. 2. Heads of state--China--Biography. I.
Title.
   DS778.M3N29 2008
   951.05092--dc22
   [B]
                              2008027829

Printed in the United States of America
First Edition

For Rose Blue, who is much missed

Contents

A Note on Spellings

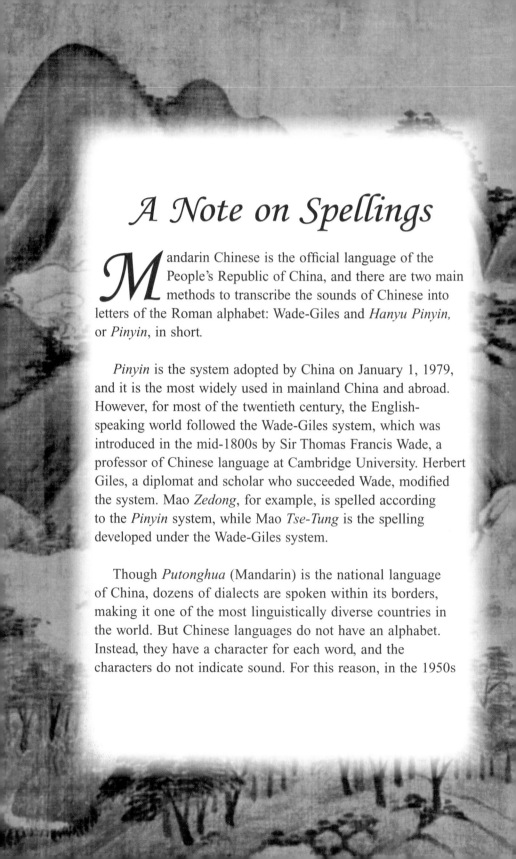

Mandarin Chinese is the official language of the People's Republic of China, and there are two main methods to transcribe the sounds of Chinese into letters of the Roman alphabet: Wade-Giles and *Hanyu Pinyin,* or *Pinyin*, in short.

Pinyin is the system adopted by China on January 1, 1979, and it is the most widely used in mainland China and abroad. However, for most of the twentieth century, the English-speaking world followed the Wade-Giles system, which was introduced in the mid-1800s by Sir Thomas Francis Wade, a professor of Chinese language at Cambridge University. Herbert Giles, a diplomat and scholar who succeeded Wade, modified the system. Mao *Zedong*, for example, is spelled according to the *Pinyin* system, while Mao *Tse-Tung* is the spelling developed under the Wade-Giles system.

Though *Putonghua* (Mandarin) is the national language of China, dozens of dialects are spoken within its borders, making it one of the most linguistically diverse countries in the world. But Chinese languages do not have an alphabet. Instead, they have a character for each word, and the characters do not indicate sound. For this reason, in the 1950s

Chinese linguists developed the fifty-eight symbol *Pinyin* system to help the Chinese people learn to read, write, and speak Mandarin. By standardizing the language, China also helped bridge the divide between the East and West; today, tens of thousands of non-native Mandarin speakers are learning the language thanks to *Pinyin*, which is considered less complex than the Wade-Giles system, with its hyphens and apostrophes.

This book, *Mao Zedong and the Cultural Revolution*, uses *Pinyin*— with a few exceptions. Wade-Giles is used for certain older names and places that have well-known English names, such as Shanghai, Chiang Kai-shek, the Kuomintang, and Peking. The origin of the name Peking is unknown; it has been attributed to Jesuits in the court of the late Chinese Ming dynasty, to British colonialists, or French missionaries in the 19th century. Whatever the origin of its name, Peking became Beiping during China's civil war; the Nationalist Party, or Kuomintang, decided to call the city Beiping, or "Northern Peace." After the Communists takeover in 1949, however, the name changed to Beijing, or the "Northern Capital." Beijing remains the city's official name, though some still refer to it as Peking.

Global map depicting the geographical relationship between the USA, Russia, and China

Mao Zedong
(Courtesy of AP Images)

one

A Land Without Pride

T he land of China is home to one of the world's oldest civilizations. Dating back, by some archeological estimations as much as 500,000 years, the country has had a dramatic history, filled with feuding warrior kings and ancient traditions. But in the twentieth century, one man reshaped China, leading it into the modern age, and defining how China would move into the future. That man was Mao Zedong, a peasant from the heartland of China who rose to become supreme leader over a country encompassing a fifth of the world's population and almost 4 million square miles.

Until the modern era, China was ruled by a series of dynasties. A dynasty was named after a person, kingdom, or the ruling family. China's recorded history began with the Shang dynasty (1523-1028 BC), coinciding with the first recorded examples of Chinese writing. For centuries after, the land was divided into warring states. Finally, in 221 BC, the Qin

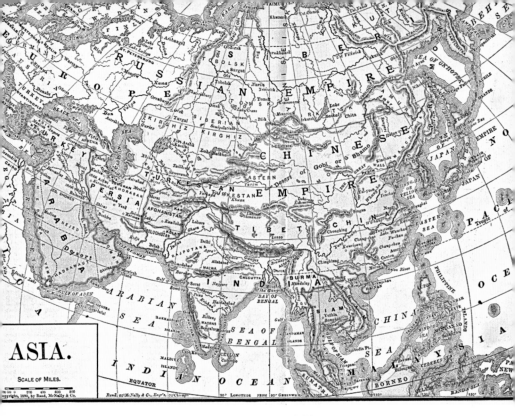

1892 map of China

dynasty conquered and united the land, setting up a strong central government and marking the beginning of imperial China.

Through the centuries, the imperial ruling system survived, even though specific dynasties died. At times, China was ruled by foreign invaders, such as the Mongols in the Yuan dynasty (AD 1279-1368). But instead of destroying the dynasty, the foreigners became part of it.

In 1644, the Manchus came south from Manchuria. They overthrew the reigning Ming rulers and founded the Qing dynasty, China's last, surviving until 1912. Although the Manchu emperors kept most Chinese customs, they made all males wear the *queue* (pigtail) as a sign of submission to the conquerors. From about 1660-1795, the Qing dynasty reached its high point.

A 1856 battle in China during the Second Opium War *(Library of Congress)*

However, early in the nineteenth century, the decline began when the government tried to stop the importation of opium into China. Great Britain and other Western nations made great profits by smuggling in the powerful and addictive narcotic drug. The Qing leaders destroyed all the foreign opium shipments at the port of Canton, sparking the Opium War of 1839-42 with Great Britain. China lost the war and was forced to sign a treaty that gave Hong Kong to the British. It also opened four new ports to British trade. Soon thereafter, the ports opened to other foreigners. A second Opium War with the British and French began in 1856, and ended in 1860 with another Chinese loss, spurring the opening of even more foreign ports.

Meanwhile, revolts hastened the decline of the dynasty from within. The most serious was the Taiping Rebellion. Rebel forces took control of most of central China in 1850 and declared their capital at Nanking. They were finally defeated in 1864.

By 1893 when Mao Zedong was born, China was sliding into one of its bleakest decades. For some time, the government had been building up its land and naval forces with modern Western-type weapons. But when the Chinese went to war with Japan in 1894 primarily over the control of Korea, they were soundly and quickly defeated by the Japanese. The fight lasted just eight months, ending in 1895. China was forced to recognize the independence of Korea and to give up Taiwan to Japan.

Three years later, young Emperor Guangxu realized the need for government reform. But his reform movement lasted just one hundred days, defeated by the conservative ruling elite.

As the twentieth century dawned, the country seethed with anti-foreign sentiment. There was a revolt by members of a Chinese secret political society called Righteous Harmony Band, who were called Boxers by Westerners who wrongly translated the name as Righteous Harmony Fists.

Encouraged by dowager empress Tz'u-his, the Righteous Harmony Band killed missionaries and tried to expel all foreigners. An army of about 16,000 troops composed of European, Japanese, Russian, and U.S. forces defeated the rebels and rescued the prisoners in 1901. The terms of the defeat were humiliating to China. Allied forces stayed in the capital of Beijing for almost a year. China had to pay more than $300 million to the victors over a period of thirty-nine years.

A battle in Tientsin, China, during the Boxer rebellion. *(Library of Congress)*

In these final days of the Chinese empire, Mao Zedong was born on December 26, 1893, in a tile-roofed house in the tiny, remote village of Shaoshan. The family name of Mao means *hair*; Zedong, means "to shine on the East." At the time of his birth, Chinese society was roughly divided into three tiers. At the top was a small group of wealthy landlords. At the bottom was most of China's population, the masses who lived in poverty and had little hope of getting out of it. In between were those often called the middle peasants who owned a few acres and had a hired worker or two.

Mao's father, Rensheng, was a middle peasant, meaning his family lived more comfortably than did most Chinese. Rensheng worked hard to become a grain dealer and farmer. He could read and write, at least enough to do his own bookkeeping. The family lived well for their surroundings, but Mao's father was a harsh and domineering man, and he frequently quarreled with his son. A slender boy with a rather high-pitched voice, Mao often rebelled against his father's commands. He said later, "I learned to hate him."

His mother, by contrast, was a gentle woman and a devout Buddhist. She had seven pregnancies, but only three—all boys—survived. "I worshipped my mother," Mao recalled. She was kind, "ever ready to share what she had," but only when her husband Rensheng was not present. "He disapproved of charity."

The Mao family may have been better off than most, but life was not easy. The village of Shaoshan, which means *magic mountain*, was isolated. Not even a newspaper kept the peasants in touch with the rest of the country. The 2,000 or so villagers lived almost in a world unto themselves. Villagers slept on hard wooden boards instead of beds. They rarely washed, and only did so in a very simplistic way, cleaning themselves with a steaming towel and rinsing their mouths with tea.

Until the age of eight, Mao lived with his mother and her family, the Wens, in a village about six miles away from Shaoshan. Adored by his maternal grandmother, two uncles and their wives, young Mao lived a carefree life.

But when Mao turned eight years old, his father arranged for him to study in a tutor's home in Shaoshan. Rensheng was mainly interested in his son's education so that he could take over the farm accounts, and eventually take over the family business.

As Mao grew older, he began attending a village school, where he was given a traditional education based on the teachings of the

Chinese philosopher Confucius—Confucianism was an offi-cial religion of China for 2,000 years. About twenty boys, ages seven or eight to about eighteen, carried a small desk and stool from their homes to the one-room building each school day. They all dressed alike: loose blue cotton jackets and baggy trousers. The teacher carried a small bamboo rod at all times, and had no qualms about using it on the students.

Though many children found Confucian classics difficult to understand, Mao had an exceptional memory and excelled at reciting and writing the ancient texts. But he didn't like the classics. Instead, he loved to read Chinese novels, or the "romances of Old China"—books like the *Three Kingdoms,* a swashbuckling narrative full of discord and chaos, rivalry and debauchery, violence and brawls.

One-hundred twenty chapters long, *Three Kingdoms* opens with the lines "the momentum of history was ever thus: The Empire long divided, must unite; long united, must divide." Within its pages mighty warriors, tyrannical generals, benev-olent rulers, corrupt government leaders, heroes with super-natural powers, and ancient Chinese beauties with "soft and jade-like skin" engage in epic battles to unite the land of China and restore peace to the country.

Mao loved these "stories of rebellion" and never grew tired of them. He would sneak and read the tales during class-time at school, "covering them up . . . when the teacher walked past." Years later, he said, "perhaps I was much influenced by such books, read at an impressionable age."

While Mao learned to read and write, quarrels between the stubborn boy and his domineering father continued— Rensheng never hesitated to scold or beat Mao for being "lazy and useless." But Mao was not one to back down. Once he ran away and threatened to jump into a pond unless his father agreed to stop the beatings. "Thus the war ended," Mao recalled, "and from it I learned that when I defended my rights by open rebellion my father relented, but when I remained meek and submissive he only cursed and beat me more."

Mao's relationships with his tutors were not much better; three teachers expelled him from school and once he ran away, claiming that the tutor was a "martinet."

When Mao was thirteen, his father Rensheng stopped paying his son's tuition fees and put him to work. Mao began to understand that he was expected to stay on the village farm for the rest of his life. Then, in an attempt to quell his son's rebellious nature by burdening him with greater responsibility, Rensheng arranged for his fourteen-year-old son to marry a cousin.

Mao never talked about this early marriage except to say that he did not want it any more than the eighteen-year-old girl did. He never considered her to be his wife, and never lived with her. She died in 1910, less than two years after they married, but Mao never got over their arranged union, calling it "a kind of indirect rape."

"In families in the West, parents acknowledge the free will of their children," he later wrote. "But in China, orders from the parents are not at all compatible with the will of the children. . . . Chinese parents are all the time indirectly raping their children."

After his wife died, Mao began to study again, this time at a private school in the village. Soon he became aware, through the books he read, that another world existed beyond the village. When he was sixteen, he told his father that he was going to enter a Western-type, higher primary school in a neighboring district, called Xiangxiang.

At the middle school in Xiangxiang township, Mao was exposed to a new world. He learned about Chinese history, and that other countries lived in different ways than did the Chinese. And he also began to learn of the reform movement led by those who wished to overthrow the current dynasty. However, although he admired the young Chinese who were calling for reform, Mao still clung to the old ways. "I considered the Emperor as well as most officials to be honest, good, and clever men," he said later. He believed that necessary reform would surely come within the system itself.

In the spring of 1911, wanting to pursue his education even further, Mao left Xiangiang, and entered middle school in the provincial capital of Changsha at the age of seventeen. He did not say goodbye to his father, and he would never again live in Shaoshan.

In Changsha, he read a newspaper for the first time, but he was not yet aware that the Qing Empire, ruled by Manch regents in the name of the six-year-old emperor, was on the edge of total collapse.

Mao was in Changsha on October 9, 1911, when a bomb exploded in the home of a Chinese army officer in Hankou, central China. The long-smoldering Chinese Revolution was about to begin. Thirty-two people were immediately arrested, and the following day, the Qing government executed three of the reform leaders. By ordering the executions, the 267-year-old ruling dynasty committed a fatal mistake.

Almost immediately there was a massive military revolt. Within a month, the revolutionary army took seventeen provinces. A new China was beginning—or so it seemed.

Mao was caught up in the excitement of revolution. He joined a number of other students in an act of defiance, cutting off their pigtails.

A member of the revolutionary forces spoke at Mao's school. After the speech, Mao was so impressed that he decided to leave at once for the city of Wuhan to join the revolution. But before Mao could leave, the revolutionary forces reached Changsha, so Mao joined them there.

The revolution in Changsha was led by two young Chinese men, Jiao Defeng, from a wealthy land-owning family, and Chen Zuoxin. Although they agreed with the basic democratic ideas of the reformists, they were more interested in helping the poor and disadvantaged. This did not sit well with Changsha's landlords and merchants. Soon isolated by local political leaders, they were killed by their own revolutionary troops. It was Mao's first lesson in the violence and betrayal that often accompanies revolutionary politics.

Mao spent about six months in the army in Changsha, doing little more than chores for the officers. Still, his fellow soldiers regarded him, at age eighteen, as an educated man, and he spent a good deal of time reading newspapers. For the first time, he encountered the word "socialism" and its theories.

Slowly, the revolutionary forces took over the country. But the child emperor did not formally give up the throne until early 1912. It seemed to Mao, however, that the reformists had a firm hand in guiding China. He later said, "Thinking the revolution was over, I resigned from the army and decided to return to my books."

The Land of China

The People's Republic of China occupies most of the habitable mainland of Asia, with a total area covering 3,705,407 square miles. It is about half the size of Russia and slightly smaller than Canada. Two-thirds of China is desert and only one-tenth is cultivated. Three great river systems water the eastern farmlands: the Yangtze, the Yellow, and Xi. The population is the world's largest, well over 1 billion people.

The head of the Chinese government is the premier, but the head of state—and the ruling power—is the head of the Communist Party. The capital city is Beijing in the northeast with a population of nearly 11 million. As a Communist country, China is officially atheist; however, some Chinese follow Buddhism, Taoism, Islam, and Christian religions.

Education is mandatory in China from ages six through fourteen. More than 90 percent of the people can read and write. That compares with literacy rates of 99 percent in Russia and the United Kingdom and 97 percent in the United States.

two
Building the Party

*I*n 1913, Mao entered the Fourth Provincial Normal
School with vague ideas of becoming a teacher. For
a while, his father agreed to pay the fees. Unsure of
his future and increasingly wary about where the revolution
was heading, Mao immersed himself in books. He learned
about the history and geography of the Western world. For
the first time, he studied maps that showed China as one
nation in proximity to other countries. Those years were a
time of learning for him and a time of great upheaval for his
country.

After the revolution, the Chinese Republic was founded in
1912. Instrumental in its founding was Sun Yat-sen, called the
father of the revolution. A graduate of the Hong Kong School
of Medicine, Sun had to flee China in 1895 because of his
revolutionary work. He toured many countries, including the
United States, to gather funds, and in 1905, he organized the
T'ung Meng Hui, a revolutionary secret society.

Sun Yat-sen was instrumental in the formation of the Chinese Republic. *(Courtesy of AP Images)*

Sun returned to China in 1911 following a successful revolution in the south. In the revolution of 1912, Qing prime minister Yuan Shih-k'ai joined the reformists. To unify the country, Sun gave up his position as provisional president of the newly formed republican government in the south. Yuan took over the country, but the new revolutionary soon proved

Soon after the Chinese Republic formed, Yuan Shih-k'ai ran the country as a dictator for more than a decade. (*Courtesy of Topical Press Agency/Getty Images*)

to be a dictator. Sun revolted against him in 1913 and formed the Kuomintang, or Nationalist Party. The revolt was unsuccessful and Sun was again driven into exile.

For more than a decade, the Chinese Republic was actually a dictatorship, running under the control of Yuan. He died in 1916, leaving China once more broken up into local regimes headed by military officers known as warlords.

Mao later recalled that during his student days, the city was overrun by troops of rival warlords. As each tried to assert authority, the brutality grew more extreme. He saw the troops rip out the eyes of peasants or burn them with kerosene. He remembered hiding in terror during an entire evening while the fighting raged at the school.

Witnessing such brutality led Mao to believe that violence was the way to achieve power. Indeed, throughout his life, he readily used brutal methods to dispose of his enemies. Later he said: "Political power grows out of the barrel of a gun."

After Mao graduated, he became a poorly paid assistant librarian in the capital city of Peking. While there, he met the library chief, Li Ta-chao, and professor of literature Chen Tu-hsui. They were both prominent Marxists.

Through Li and Chen, Mao became acquainted with the theories of Marxism. With his country still in turmoil, he began to believe that China must experience a deep social and political revolution in order to survive.

In early 1919, Mao heard that his mother, suffering from inflammation of the lymph glands and diphtheria, had taken a turn for the worse. He met her and his younger brothers in Changsha where she was seeking treatment. The treatment failed and she died in October. His father died of typhoid a few months later.

After his return to Peking, Mao became more and more entwined with the Marxists at his school. Then, on May 4, 1919, an uprising led to the founding of the Chinese Communist Party (CCP). It started from news that the Treaty of Versailles, which formally ended World War I, ignored China's demands to retake the territory lost to Japan during the war. Thousands

Karl Marx *(Library of Congress)*

of students and young intellectuals flooded the streets in an outpouring of rage and shame. Mao was among them. The crowd ran through Tiananmen Square to the missions of the Americans, British, French, and Italians, and finally to the building of the foreign ministry. They set the last on fire.

This massive protest came to be known as the May Fourth Incident. It spread to every corner of China, creating great resentment against the government and

Marxism

German political philosopher Karl Marx (1818-83) introduced the theory of Marxism, which he called *scientific socialism* or *communism.* Conflict between the social classes, said Marx, is inevitable. One class will be dominant over the other. The exploited class will at some time overthrow the oppressors—only to become the next oppressor. The final conflict can happen only when the *proletariat,* working class, overthrows the *bourgeoisie,* the property owners.

According to Marx, after the final conflict revolution, the proletariat will become a dictator, with all means of production under the government. Gradually, however, all class conflict will end and society will become classless and Communist.

Mao (far right) with his mother and two younger brothers in 1919.
(Courtesy of Gamma/Eyedea/ZUMA Press)

Japan, and set off a massive cry for cultural, social, and political change. For the first time, Mao wrote a journal article in which he claimed to speak of the masses (a term he used extensively throughout his career). He said later of this period: "It was by this time I had become in theory, and, to some extent, in action, a Marxist."

In late December 1919, Mao began work as director of a Peking primary school. For the first time, he had a respectable job and income. This enabled him to marry Yang Kaihui, the daughter of his former professor. She was a slight girl with a pale complexion. Their marriage was still rather unique in China since it was the free choice of both parties, and Yang was an unconventional Chinese wife. "Women are human beings, just as men are . . . Sisters!" she wrote in an essay. "We must fight for the equality of men and women, and must absolutely not allow people to treat us as an accessory." Mao and Yang settled into family life, and had three sons: Anying, Anching, and Anlong.

During 1920 and 1921, Mao wrote many newspaper articles on his growing commitment to Marxist ideals and communism. He was part of the study group and informal network set up by Li and Chen. Other informal groups spread around China.

The Chinese Communist Party (CCP) began under the guidance of Soviet Russia. CCP leaders saw the Russian Revolution of 1917 as a model for their own goals. In 1919, the Soviets formed an international Communist organization called the Comintern. It sent delegates to see Li and Chen to lay plans for a communist party in China.

The official founding of the CCP took place in Shanghai in June 1921. The First Congress was attended by twelve men; Mao was one of two delegates from Hunan. His participation was minor. Li and Chen, the party's founders, were unable to attend. Chen, however, was named the head of the new party. With about fifty members, it was a small beginning for a group that would eventually become the largest political party in the world. (The CCP today is estimated at 70 million members.)

With the help of the Comintern, the CCP gradually increased its membership. By the mid-1920s, two major revolutionary groups were contending for power in China:

the Kuomintang, or Nationalists, led by Sun Yat-sen, and the CCP. Mao's importance to the CCP was growing. He became the secretary of the Hunan branch and devoted himself to building up the tiny following. Meanwhile, Sun Yat-sen, with money and equipment from the Soviets, established the Whampoa Academy to train officers for the new Kuomintang army. At its head he installed a young officer named Chiang Kai-shek.

In 1924, the Communists joined Sun's Kuomintang (KMT) with the idea of carrying out a so-called northern expedition to bring all of China under its control. But Sun died in March of that year, leaving the Kuomintang's leadership open. It was filled by Chiang Kai-shek, who became the most important figure in the organization. By this time, Mao was an active member in the KMT. He was so zealous in his work that his own CCP members criticized him for being too devoted.

The northern expedition proceeded and by early 1926, half of China was under KMT control. It looked as though Chiang and his forces would succeed in their goal. However, the union of the KMT and the Communists was not as solid as it seemed. Marx, who believed in revolution by the workers, regarded peasants as "the class that represents barbarism in the midst of civilization." But Mao had spent the last few years in the midst of the peasants, trying to get membership for the CCP. In 1927, he wrote one of his most famous articles, entitled The Report on the Peasant Movement in Hunan. Slowly, he was coming to see that it was the peasants, not the workers, who were the key to revolution. The peasants would take power from the landlords. If they did not, no one else would. The struggle against imperial rule rested solely with them.

Chiang Kai-shek, the most important figure in the Kuomintang after Sun's death. *(Courtesy of AP Images/CNA Photo)*

By acknowledging the overthrow of the landlords by the peasants, Mao caused much anxiety among CCP leaders. The CCP had many landlord allies. In addition, many of the Kuomingtang officers were from landlord backgrounds. As a result, the party published only the first two parts of Mao's essay in its official party publication, called *Xiangdao (The Guide)*. Unpublished was the part that described the peasant execution of landlords.

With his growing belief, Mao separated himself from the Marxist view of the workers' revolution. As the CCP became more powerful (by early 1925, it expanded to more than 57,000), Mao thought it could take over control of the KMT and, eventually, the country.

However, Chiang believed that too. So, in April 1927, he ordered a counter-revolutionary campaign. The aim was to massacre Communists and militant workers in the cities. In Changsha, soldiers marched the streets, murdering students and unionists in the name of Chiang. Nearly 30,000 people died in Hunan, and membership in the CCP dropped from 60,000 to 10,000.

By this time, Mao controlled about 3,000 peasants in the Hunan area. Leaders of the CCP, with the support of the Comintern representative, planned an assault against the Kuomintang on September 7, 1927. Known as the Autumn Harvest Uprising, an insurrection took place in several cities in the provinces of Hunan and Jiangxi. This was the first armed rebellion by the Communists. Mao led an attack in the uprising and expected that the peasants, as Marx predicted, would rise and conquer.

Instead, the losses were severe. Within in a week, Mao was forced to draw back his men, now numbering about one

Mao in 1925, around the time he began to build up a small following in the CCP. (*Courtesy of Getty Images*)

thousand. Most were untrained soldiers, and they often ended up fighting each other. Some deserted. Mao himself was captured during a skirmish and barely managed to escape. He later said that at this point he learned the importance of having political goals backed up by adequate military forces.

With the insurrection a failure, Mao established a guerilla base in a remote region on the Hunan-Jiangxi border called Jinggangshan. It was later known as "Sacred Mountain of the Revolution." Mao's wife, Yang, and their sons did not go to the mountain base with him. Instead, they stayed behind.

During the next few months, ensconced on the mountain, Mao began to show the unwavering will and determination that marked the rest of his career. He had a plan to ensure future insurrections wouldn't end in failure: the rebel forces must never again be undefended, therefore, the Communist Party must become an army for a time. A strong army would soon control the countryside and from there could capture the cities. The cities would fall as the last, not the first, act of the revolution. It was not Marxism as preached by the master or as practiced in Russia. It was not Marxism at all, but a new political strategy that would come to be known as Maoism.

Until this point, Mao had never written much about military power. He did not look like nor act like a military man. But now he built an army. A deal with bandit chiefs got him rifles and fighting men, who joined a growing army of drifters, deserters from the Kuomintang, thieves, and downtrodden peasants. Mao set up classes for soldiers to learn military tactics and for peasants to learn to read and write.

Officially called the Chinese Workers' and Peasants' Red Army, Mao's militia was modeled on the Russian Soviet system. Each squad had a party group and each company had a party branch. All were under control of the Front Committee, with Mao as secretary. This force was run differently from the traditional Chinese army. Instead of forcing people to serve, the Red Army was an all-volunteer force; if a soldier wanted to leave, he was given money for the trip home. Officers were not permitted to beat the volunteer soldiers, who were even promised a grievance committee in the case of assault or wrongdoing. Rules also stipulated that civilians had to be treated fairly by the army. Soldiers had to pay a fair price for what they bought from civilians and were required to speak politely in the exchange.

Mao stayed in the hills with his ragtag band, planning and building his strategy. In 1930, he was thirty-seven years old, and spent much of his time working diligently to establish the peasant rebellion. In doing so, he often scorned the advice of the Comintern representative and rejected orders from Moscow. The Russians repeatedly urged that he base his activities in the towns instead of the countryside. Mao ignored them.

It was around this time that news reached Mao that his wife Yang and their eight-year-old son Anying had been captured by the Nationalists. They demanded that Yang publicly denounce Mao, and say they were divorced. She refused, and was executed. His son was released, and along with his two brothers, eventually taken to a CCP school by Mao's allies.

By the time of Yang's death, Mao already considered himself divorced from her; in 1927, he had met He Zizhen, the seventeen-year-old daughter of a communist bookseller. Mao promptly made her his third wife. A former school teacher and Communist organizer, He Zizhen served him as a loyal member of the CCP. Still, Mao was distraught over the death of Yang Kaihui, his estranged wife. "The death of Kaihui cannot be redeemed by a hundred deaths of mine!" he said. Throughout the remainder of his life,

Mao spoke of Yang in kind, loving terms, especially as he got older.

During the years of hiding out, and following the death of his second wife, Mao revealed a growing ruthlessness. It became particularly apparent during The Futian Incident of December 1930. Under Mao's orders, some 4,000 troops whom Mao regarded as rebels were tortured and executed, women and men. A document covering such activities, with the approval of Mao, warned that important leaders were not to be killed too quickly. Instead, they should be slowly tortured, in order to force them to give up useful information before they died.

To Mao's way of thinking, "a brief reign of terror" was a practical and necessary evil. In a report he authored on the peasant movement, Mao wrote that "a revolution is not the same as inviting people to dinner or writing an essay or painting a picture or embroidering a flower; it cannot be anything so refined, so calm and gentle, or so mild, kind, courteous, restrained and magnanimous. A revolution is an uprising, an act of violence whereby one class overthrows the authority of another."

Mao was a long way from becoming the leader of his country. But his policies and tactics were taking hold. And it was there on the Sacred Mountain of the Revolution that the lessons of the abortive insurrection were studied and absorbed. It was there that a new strategy for revolution emerged.

Building an Army of Peasants

*I*n 1928, Chiang Kai-shek became chairman of the Nationalist government that had at least nominal control over most of the country. The capital was established at Nanking. Soon, the Nationalists captured Peking and renamed it Peiping.

In the meantime, Mao stayed hidden at his base in the hills. Little by little, he broadened and perfected his strategy for revolution. Mao's approach was simple, direct, and effective. He had his men search out the small villages in the surrounding countryside one by one. Once they entered a village, they gathered the landlords in a central meeting place. There, the crimes of the landlords were discussed with the village peasants. Then the peasants executed the landlords, all under the supervision of the Red Army. With the landlords gone, their farms were distributed among the peasants. Besides pleasing the peasants, the technique also got recruits for the Red Army.

In this manner, by February 1930, Mao declared himself in charge of the South-West Soviet-Provincial Government.

However, Chiang's forces had defeated nearly all the northern warlords by this time. His government seemed stable, so much so that these years are often called the Nationalist Decade. Yet, Chiang's leadership was weakened in part by his half-hearted response to Japanese aggression in 1931. Japan invaded and occupied Manchuria on China's eastern seaboard in the so-called Manchurian Incident. Despite the obvious indication that Japan wanted to expand, Chiang

Japanese troops entering Manchuria in 1931. *(Courtesy of Keystone/Getty Images)*

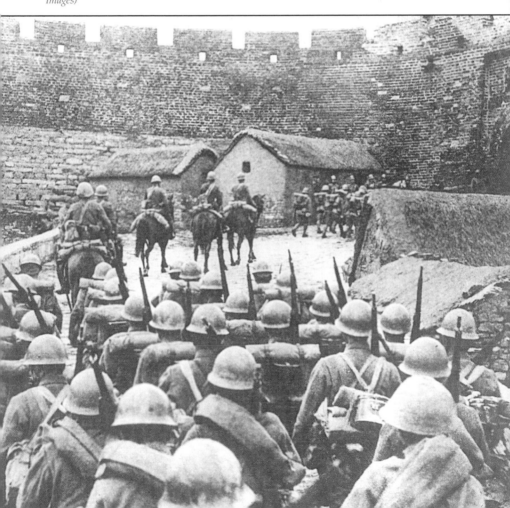

Kai-shek remained convinced that it was in China's best interests to avoid full-scale war.

Indeed, Chiang was much more concerned with defeating the Communists than thwarting Japanese aggression, but he was not having much success. To stop the growth of CCP membership and expansion of its territory, Chiang ordered the first of five so-called encirclement campaigns. The aim was to surround the Red forces and cut them off from each other.

The First Encirclement Campaign took place between November 1930 and January 3, 1931, in southern Jiangxi. Chiang commanded some 100,000 Nationals against Mao's 40,000 Red Army soldiers. Chiang's plan was to launch multiple attacks on the main Communist base at Jiangxi.

At first, the Communist leaders disagreed about how to defend themselves, but Mao began developing and arguing for guerilla tactics to fight Chiang's large army. He summarized his strategy with slogans such as "The enemy advances, we retreat; the enemy halts, we harass; the enemy tires, we attack; the enemy retreats, we pursue."

Mao successfully argued that the Red troops should stay within the Jiangxi and help defend the base with the support of the people. The tactic worked. By late December, five Nationalist divisions were ordered into the heart of the Jiangxi encampment to begin a general offensive. By December 30, the campaign was over. The divisions were wiped out by the Communists, and the Red Army pursed the enemy and launched its own attack on January 3.

The result was a decisive victory for the Red Army. Chiang lost more than 15,000 troops as well as some 12,000 guns and artilleries.

The Second Encirclement Campaign, in April 1931, also ended in a Red Army victory. This time, the Nationals led by He Yingqin intended to encircle the Jiangxi Soviet base with some 200,000 soldiers and destroy it. The 30,000-man Red Army was led by Zhu De. Again, they repelled the Nationalist attack and launched their own counter-campaign. The Nationals lost about 30,000 men.

In less than a month, Chiang ordered the Third Encirclement Campaign. This time he had the advice of British, Japanese, and German military leaders who had arrived at Nanchang. But the result was the same, and the Nationalists lost another 30,000 men.

Chiang again tried to destroy the Red Army in the Fourth Encirclement campaign, which lasted from December 1931 to March 21, 1932. He led nearly 500,000 men in another attack against Jiangxi. Mao and other generals led the Red Army force of about 70,000. Again, the Communists were victorious, but this battle was not as easily won and their losses were considerable.

Chiang was not to be defeated, though. He launched the the Fifth Encirclement campaign on September 25, 1933. This time, he had a force of about 1 million Nationalists (some borrowed from warlords), and he led them to the Communist base at Jiangxi, defended by about 130,000 Red Army soldiers.

As Chiang gathered his massive army, a militant group within the CCP forced Mao out of the leadership position, replacing him with a three-man committee. The committee abandoned Mao's mobile warfare tactics in favor of direct confrontation. But Chiang, following his German advisors, ordered his troops to encircle the Jiangxi region with fortified blockhouses. Stubbornly, the Communists kept trying to attack the blockhouses without success. By October 1934, the Red Army had lost the fight, more than 40,000 men, and their largest base in China.

With success in the fifth encirclement campaign, Chiang achieved an important milestone in consolidating his rule in eastern China. The way seemed clear for him to reach total victory: full and complete control of the country. Now he could finish off the remaining CCP forces, get rid of the rest of the warlords, and then take back Manchuria from the Japanese.

Defeated by Chiang and facing starvation, the Red Army had little choice but to break through Nationalist lines. The idea was to retreat to the north-west and regroup forces. Thus began the Long March. This massive military retreat was actually several long marches as a number of Communist armies escaped. The most well known, however, was the march from Jiangxi province in October 1934. Mao and Zhou Enlai, who was also instrumental in the rise of the Chinese Communist Party, led the First Front Army of about 30,000 troops. They traveled more than 6,000 miles, across eighteen mountain ranges, twenty-four rivers, and several deserts—their journey took one year.

The march was a nightmare—day after day of pain and death. The retreating forces carried weapons, artillery, party files, and any equipment that would help them set up a new base. Constant attacks by the Nationalist air force and artillery units decimated the columns. But the marchers continued even though there was no definite decision on where they were going, what direction, or how precisely to get there.

In January 1935, the Communists took the city of Zunyi, where party leaders held a conference. The army and the

Members of the CCP army during the Long March in 1935. *(Courtesy of Three Lions/Getty Images)*

party were in disarray; poor decision making was the main cause of the failure of the fifth encirclement. Those leaders were denounced, and Mao's prestige grew. He was elected one of three members of the Military Affairs Commission. Because the other two, Zhou Enlai and Wang Jiaxiang, were not considered superior in military affairs, Mao in effect now headed the First Red Army.

Zhou Enlai in 1925 *(Courtesy of AFP/Getty Images)*

Poetry by Mao

It may seem unusual in a dedicated political and military leader but Mao Zedong was also a poet. He composed many poems throughout his lifetime, and most are considered to be well written. Much of his work is still popular in China. One of his most well-known poems is *The Long March* written in October 1935 when the journey was almost finished. It reads:

The Red Army fears not the trials of the March,

Holding light ten thousand crags and torrents.

The Five Ridges wind like gentle ripples

And the majestic Wumeng roll by, globules of clay.

Warm the steep cliffs lapped by the waters of Golden Sand,

Cold the iron chains spanning the Tatu River,

Minshan's thousand li of snow joyously crossed,

The three Armies march on, each face glowing.

Traveling north once again, Mao and his men crossed the Yangtze on May 8, 1935, with the army down to about 25,000. Now they had to fight not only the Nationalists but local warlord allies as well. Casualties resulted from these military encounters, in addition to the hunger, cold, sickness, and extreme fatigue. Many soldiers deserted.

Mao's First Army reached the Shaanxi province in October, and established a headquarters in a cave. By the next October, the other army divisions had reached Shaanxi as well, and the Long March officially came to an end.

Though the march was successful in relocating the Red Army, it came with heavy costs. The journey began with about 87,000 soldiers; by the end, only about 10,000 remained alive. Although a tragic loss of life, the Long March was a personal triumph for Mao, who regained the prestige he had lost among party leaders. The march also announced to Chiang Kai-shek that the Red Army would not be easily defeated. Mao wrote at the end of the march: "The Long March is a manifesto. It has proclaimed to the world that the Red Army is an army of heroes, while the imperialists and their running dogs, Chiang Kai-shek and his like, are impotent."

Edgar Snow

American journalist Edgar Snow gave the world its first public account of Mao in the 1937 book *Red Star Over China*. Until then, no foreign observer had made contact with or interviewed Mao. Snow traveled by truck, train, on foot, and astride a horse with a "quarter-moon back and a camel gait" to reach Mao and his Red Army troops at Yenan, the end point of the Long March. A correspondent for several influential publications, including the *Saturday Evening Post, Chicago Tribune,* and *London Daily Herald,* Snow spent five months conducting interviews with Mao at his lamp-lit cave. There, Mao served Snow hot-peppered bread and sour plum compote, and Snow wrote that he found Mao "a gaunt, rather Lincolnesque figure, above average height for a Chinese, somewhat stooped, with a head of thick black hair grown very long, and with large searching eyes, a high-bridged nose and prominent cheekbones."

Snow's account also described Mao as a man with "a deep sense of personal dignity," and seemingly "quite free from symptoms of megalomania." He added that "something about him suggests a power of ruthless decision."

Because Snow had unprecedented personal access to Mao, as well as other key figures in the guerilla movement that brought the Community Party of China to power in 1949, *Red Star Over China* and his newspaper dispatches remain essential reading. Snow is the only Western journalist, for example, that Mao ever spoke to about his arranged marriage to his cousin.

In recent years, however, Snow and his writings have come under close scrutiny by leading China scholars and historians. Critics characterize Snow's reporting as naïve and sympathetic to the Chinese Communists. Worse, some argue that Snow introduced Mao as a hero to the West, creating a favorable but misleading and false view of the guerilla leader. They say Mao used Snow to spread misinformation and propaganda, with the result that nearly all subsequent accounts of Mao and the beginnings of the Chinese Communist movement have relied on Snow's writings as *the* primary source.

Snow reported, for example, that Mao remained true to his peasant roots during his time in Yenan. "He owned only his blankets and a few personal belongings, including two cotton uniforms." New documentation has revealed that Mao owned more than fifty lavish personal estates throughout China during his twenty-seven year rule. One of those residences was in Yenan, where Snow first met Mao—Mao even had the house outfitted with central wall heating, a rare luxury for homes at that time.

Even aspects of the Long March have been called into question by recent scholarship. It's now known that at least one alleged bridge attack never occurred. Similarly, new findings suggest that Mao did not suffer on the march. At least two leading Mao scholars maintain that he spent much of his time reading books, while being carried on a litter by porters.

For his part, Snow continued to make trips to China throughout his life. His last trip was in 1969-70, two years before U.S. President Richard Nixon made his historic 1972 visit to improve relations between the U.S. and China. Snow died in Switzerland on February 15, 1972, and some of his ashes are buried at Beijing University, where he once taught.

Time will tell how historians and scholars ultimately choose to regard Snow, but most will agree that some of Snow's initial impressions of Mao proved right, at least in one respect. In *Red Star Over China*, Snow wrote that he "felt a certain force of destiny in Mao . . ." He added, "Mao Tse-Tung might possibly become a very great man."

An Edgar Snow memorial in Beijing, China. *(Courtesy of johnrochaphoto/Alamy)*

中國人民的美國朋友
埃德加·斯諾
之墓
葉劍英 一九七七年十二月十三日

IN MEMORY OF EDGAR SNOW
AN AMERICAN FRIEND OF THE CHINESE PEOPLE
1905—1972

four

The Fight for Communism

apan and China had quarreled in the First Sino-Japanese War (1894-1895), when Japan defeated the Qing dynasty. China had to give up Taiwan and recognize the independence of Korea. In the following years, numerous incidents marked a fight for territory between China and Japan. But with Chiang Kai-shek's eye on the Communists, Japan was able to invade Manchuria in 1931 in the so-called Mukden Incident, when a train track near the city of Mukden in South Manchuria was bombed. The Japanese blamed Chinese saboteurs, while others suggest the bombing was a carefully orchestrated Japanese plan to provide a pretext for the Japanese invasion of Manchuria. Japan established the puppet state of Manchukuo in Manchuria and pressed China to recognize it. China appealed to the League of Nations, which condemned Japan. In response, Japan withdrew from the League. But in 1933 and 1935, Japan forced China to establish two demilitarized zones bordering Manchuria.

By this time, many Chinese were frustrated with Chiang's unwillingness or inability to confront Japan's aggression directly. As a result, in December 1936 when Chiang was inspecting troops in the northeast, he was arrested and kidnapped by one of his young generals.

Mao surprised both Chiang's followers and his own by pleading for Chiang's life, declaring that the two warring factions must be united to defeat Japan. This was a smart move by Mao. He could not have defeated Japan alone, and he showed that Japan's defeat and the survival of the Chinese nation was the greater priority than the civil conflicts that had been dividing the nation. Chiang was forced to agree to a shaky union with the CCP to fight the Japanese as a condition of his release.

But on July 7, 1937, Japanese troops began crossing the Marco Polo Bridge, near Peking. Kuomintang soldiers tried to hold them off, but to little avail, and before long, the Japanese marched to Peking. Most experts mark this, the Marco Polo Bridge Incident, as the beginning of the Second Sino-Japanese War, which, in China, is also known as the War of Resistance Against Japan.

With Japanese forces advancing into China, Chiang had little choice but to accept Communist troops into the National Revolutionary Army. The Red Army became the Eighth Route Army and the rest of the CCP guerrilla forces became the New Fourth Army.

This alliance allowed the Communists to expand their troops, power, and influence. Mao's own prestige and power were also on the rise. He was not yet the top leader of his

Japanese troops attacking Chinese defenders during the Second Sino-Japanese War. *(Courtesy of AP Images)*

party, but his skills and diplomacy had not gone unnoticed. He especially caught the eye of Josef Stalin, the Communist leader of the U.S.S.R, who regarded Mao's ideas as closest to his own.

As war raged between the Chinese and the Japanese's army, which numbered around 350,000 men, Chiang struggled to defeat the foreign invaders and keep Mao and the CCP from gaining too much power. Mao had the upper hand, though. Japan used its manpower to attack Chiang's armies in the cities and on the transportation routes, leaving the countryside—and Mao's peasants—relatively untouched.

Japan scored easy victories in northern China, but in August there was a major standstill between the two forces

Josef Stalin, the Communist leader of the U.S.S.R., supported Mao and the CCP. *(Library of Congress)*

in Shanghai. Chiang, anxious to show Japan, the world, and his people that he would not allow the Japanese to simply take China, decided to make a stand at Shanghai instead of a fast retreat to save casualties. He sent the best of his troops—German-trained divisions—into the battle. The battle for Shanghai waged on for three months, and China was defeated, but it showed that the troops could and would fight.

However, the fighting was vicious and the casualties many. Both sides were left with a deep loathing for one another and a vow for vengeance. Some historians say that it was the principal reason for the Nanking Massacre in December 1937. The Japanese were victorious there too, and some 300,000 people died in the massacre that followed the fall of the city.

Meanwhile, the uneasy alliance between Chiang's and Mao's troops began to break down. In truth, the alliance between troops of Chiang and Mao was never unified because each was getting ready to fight the other as soon as Japan was defeated. Communists tried to win over the public with mass demonstrations and tax and administrative reforms that favored the peasants, and frequent fighting broke out between the Communists and the Nationalists outside the areas of Japanese control.

By late 1938, Japan had made steady gains in northern China, the rich Yangtze River valley, and the coastal regions. And in 1939, when World War II began with Nazi Germany invading Poland, Japan allied itself with the Nazis and the Italian fascists in a bid for even more land and power. Japan bombed Pearl Harbor on December 7, 1941, bringing the United States into the war. China officially declared war on Japan the next day; it had not done so before because it was afraid neutral nations would stop their aid. Now, much of the world was united against Japan and its allies, and Chiang became certain that Japan would be wholly defeated. He no longer merely sought survival for his country; he sought a great victory over Japan.

China quickly found itself allied with superpowers such as the U.S. and the U.S.S.R. Enriched with foreign money, better trained, and better equipped, the Chinese army aggressively fought back against the Japanese.

During the years of war against Japan, Mao's personal life was undergoing significant changes. He had grown apart from his third wife He Zizhen; she had bore him five children, four of which had died or been left behind with peasant families on the Long March. He Zizhen suspected Mao of having affairs with other women—and she was right. Mao had become particularly interested in a young woman named Jiang Qing.

Mao met Qing in 1937. Qing was born in 1914, the daughter of a concubine and an inn-owner. Her father was an alcoholic, and frequently abusive, but young Qing was strong-willed and brave, frequently fighting back when her father hit her mother. Her mother encouraged Qing's willfulness, even allowing her to unbind her feet at age six (Chinese women of the time had a custom of binding the feet of young girls, breaking the bones to prevent the foot from growing too large). Qing's willfulness grew into obstinacy; at age twelve, she was expelled from school and at the age of fourteen, she ran away from home to join a traveling opera troupe.

It was when she was performing at the Peking Opera in the city of Yenan that Qing met Mao. Mao had recently moved to that city, and was quick to patronize the Peking Opera, one of his favorite pastimes. He was instantly attracted to Qing, and she worked hard to return his attentions, attending his lectures and asking many questions. Before long, they began a relationship, frequently appearing together in public.

Soon, it became clear that Mao wanted to marry Qing, but his closest friends and advisors warned him it was a mistake.

Mao and Jiang Qing in 1936 *(Courtesy of Fox Photos/Getty Images)*

Some worried about how it would look for the chairman to leave his wife, who was ill at the time. Many even wrote letters to Mao; one letter writer remembers that the letters "went roughly like this: Chairman Mao, we hope you won't marry Jiang Qing. [Your wife] is in very poor health, and you have had five or six children together." Then, they added, "Jiang Qing's reputation is pretty bad."

Indeed, it was Qing's reputation and history that raised the most concerns amongst Mao's colleagues. Years earlier, Qing had been arrested and imprisoned by the Nationalists; though this in itself was typical, many suspected that she had arranged her release by signing a recantation of Communist ideals, an act considered to be a betrayal by the CCP. She was also rumored to have been a sexual companion to the guards while in jail.

Mao was not to be deterred, though. After receiving messages warning him against marrying Qing, Mao exclaimed to a messenger, "I will get married . . . Everyone else can mind their own business!" Mao quickly got his security chief Kang Sheng to vouch for Qing, though it was likely that both men knew the charges against her were true. Mao's insistence and Sheng's advocacy were enough to silence Qing's critics, and the two were married in 1937.

He Zizhen learned about Mao's marriage to Qing from an article, while in Moscow. Pregnant with Mao's sixth child, she had traveled there to get medical treatment for shrapnel wounds suffered during a bombing raid on the Long March. There, she gave birth to a little boy, but he died of pneumonia a few months later. Mao insisted that He Zizhen stay in Moscow. He told her they were no longer married, "only comrades."

He Zizhen never fully recovered, physically or emotionally, from all that had happened; she was committed to a psychiatric institution for a time. But she eventually was reunited with her daughter with Mao, Chiao-Chiao (or Li Min), who she had left behind when she went to Moscow.

In 1943, Mao was named chairman of the Communist Central Committee and chairman of the Politburo. Shortly afterward, the Soviet Union dissolved the Comintern, but Mao remained respectful to Stalin.

While Mao lived in Yenan, American advisory groups visited him to explore ways in which the Communist troops could be used more effectively. As always, he charmed his visitors with his earthy ways and an easy laugh. And as always, he spoke of his peasant society against the exploitation of the landlords. In this manner, a sort of cult of personality was developing around Mao. He spoke of himself as an enemy of imperialism, landowners, and businessmen, a friend to the farmers, workers, and above all, the peasants. Later in life, Mao said that personality cults were desirable as long as they honored someone who deserved it, someone like Marx or Stalin. Blind worship, he said, was false. Over the years and little by little, the Chinese people would come to believe in and follow not only Mao's direction but his thoughts and beliefs as well.

This became clear in mid-1945 when the Seventh Party Congress met in Yenan. A new preamble to the party's constitution was presented. It said: "The Chinese Communist Party takes Mao Zedong's thought—the thought that unites Marxist-Lenist theory and the practice of the Chinese Revolution—as the guide for all its work, and opposes all dogmatic or empiricist deviations." In other words, what Mao thought, the rest of China was supposed to think as well.

Mao Zedong

At the end of World War II, the United States gave most of its Eastern surplus war materials to Chiang. Mao received captured equipment from the Russians, who had taken it from 700,000 Japanese soldiers fleeing Manchuria.

Following the U.S. atomic bombing of the Japanese cities Hiroshima and Nagasaki, the Japanese surrendered, ending World War II. Troops in China formally surrendered on September 9, 1945. For being on the winning side of the global conflict, China regained Manchuria, Taiwan, and the Pescadores, a group of islands in the Formosa Strait.

In 1945, though China had emerged victorious from World War II and its conflict with Japan, the nation was economically nearly destroyed and on the verge of civil war. Millions were homeless. Towns and cities in many parts of the country were devastated. In addition, Chiang Kai-shek faced a nation growing increasingly angry with his policies. In contrast, through hard work and by appealing to people's desire for a change, the CCP increased its membership from 100,000 in 1937 to 1.2 million in 1945.

That December in 1945, U.S. General George Marshall went to China hoping to build a coalition government with the Nationalists and Communists. But neither Chiang's representatives nor Zhou Enlai, who was representing the Communists, was willing to compromise on certain issues or give up any land they had taken. The truce fell apart in the spring of 1946, and Marshall went home the following January. What the country had been inevitably building toward finally came to pass. With the breakdown of talks and the departure of Marshall, all-out civil war began.

Initially, Chiang was winning, his armies proving victorious in Hunan, Hubei, and Manchuria. As the generalissimo

General George Marshall traveled to China in 1945, hoping to negotiate peace between the Nationalists and the CCP. *(Library of Congress)*

(commander in chief) of the Chinese forces, he was aided by the United States—which, with the Cold War beginning, didn't want to see China fall to Communists. They poured in millions of dollars worth of military supplies and equipment, and airlifted Nationalist troops from central China to Manchuria. The Soviet Union gave some aid to the Communists, but it was modest compared to the help from the United States.

☭ Mao Zedong

In 1948, Chiang became the first president of China to be chosen through a constitution. However, in that year, the Nationalists began to lose ground militarily. Chiang, willing to try anything to hold onto his power and defeat the CCP, resigned the presidency to take charge of the army, but his forces were spread too thin. The Communists, adept at both guerilla warfare and larger scale battles involving mobile formations, quickly defeated the worn out Nationalist army. By late that year, Communists troops—now renamed the People's Liberation Army (PLA)—controlled much of northern China.

Mao predicted that the Nationalist attacks would crumble, but even he was surprised at the speed with which his enemies fell. By the end of March 1948, the PLA took most of Manchuria and cities to the south. Yenan fell on April 25. On January 31, 1949, Peking was taken without a fight, and renamed Beijing. Then, on April 21, the capital of the Nationalist's Republic of China fell. As the PLA drove south, Chiang moved the Nationalist capital to Canton.

On October 1, 1949, Mao, addressed a crowd in Beijing's famous Tiananmen Square, and officially declared the establishment of the People's Republic of China. Solidifying himself as the man who would lead China into the future, Mao said: "The Chinese people have stood up . . . nobody will insult us again."

The Nationalist capital Canton fell on October 15, forcing Chiang to withdraw his army. About 600,000 troops and 2 million refugees, most from the government and business communities, left the Chinese mainland for the nearby island of Taiwan, leaving only small pockets of Nationalist resistance, mainly in the south.

Mao formally announcing the establishment of the People's Republic of China in Tiananmen Square, on Oct. 1, 1949. *(Courtesy of AP Images)*

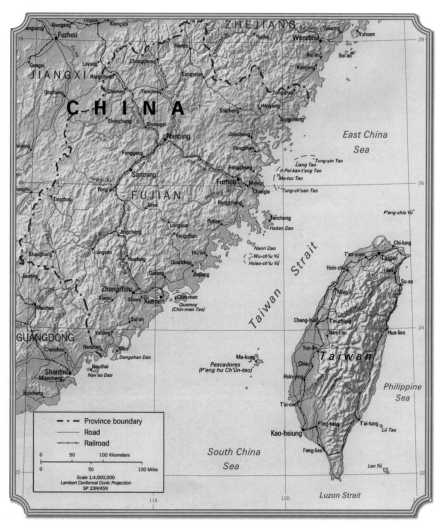

A modern map of Taiwan

Taiwan, also called Formosa, lies some one hundred miles off the southeast Chinese mainland. In December, Chiang proclaimed Taipei, Taiwan, as the temporary capital of the Republic of China. Once again assuming the presidency, he declared his government to be China's legitimate authority.

Backed by U.S. aid, he announced his intention of returning to the mainland to recapture the country.

That never happened, though Chiang did turn Taiwan into a prosperous nation by carrying out extensive industrialization. During the few years prior to his death in 1975, his son, Chiang Ching-kuo, ran the government as premier.

The last of the fighting between the Communists and the Nationalist took place in May 1950 when the Communists captured Hainan Island. Mao Zedong, aged fifty-six, had already turned his attention to the enormous task at hand. He would build a new nation dedicated to socialist principles. Eventually, the world would know, respect, and fear his philosophy as Maoism.

five

Creating the People's Republic

rom 1949 until his death in 1976—Mao Zedong was viewed as a living god by the Chinese people. This was not merely blind worship. Mao brought them victory and respect, and he freed them from years of humiliation at the hands of foreigners. He promised to bring them a better life.

But in 1949, the new leader of the old country faced enormous problems. China had been in turmoil for nearly four decades. The country was in disarray. The economy was in shambles: there was no unified currency and no administrative structure, and inflation was out of control. Sunken ships filled the harbors, and millions of people had no homes. Schools and universities had no books and few teachers. Out of this chaos, Mao faced the staggering task of changing every institution in China, political or not, into a socialist form.

Mao ran the government, although he did not always do so alone. During these rebuilding years, at times Mao was voted out of top party leadership, which meant he was not the head of state. At other times, he shared the responsibility. But overall, it was Mao's philosophy, ruthlessness, and determination that shaped China and turned it into a world power.

His first order was to bring stability and unity to the splintered nation. All opposition to the ruling Communist Party was outlawed. In fact, all other political parties were outlawed. Mao's new government would expect—and receive—total obedience.

On the day following Mao's declaration of the People's Republic (October 1, 1949), the Soviet Union was the first to officially recognize the new Communist nation. Shortly after, Mao made plans for his first trip outside his country, to meet with Communist Party leaders. In December 1949, he left for Moscow, his first look at a non-Chinese society, and a meeting with seventy-year-old Joseph Stalin, the dictator of the U.S.S.R.

Mao was always respectful of Stalin, his ideas, and his place in Communist history. But Stalin viewed Mao much like a new pupil who should follow in the teacher's footsteps. Mao, in contrast, felt his military victory placed him on equal footing with anyone. During one visit, Stalin kept Mao waiting so long for an appointment that the Chinese leader threatened to leave Moscow. He did not because Mao needed the Soviet Union to buffer any further threat from Japan and for the offered $300 million in aid. This came in the form of a Treaty of Friendship, Alliance, and Mutual Assistance.

When Stalin died in 1953, Mao called him: "The greatest genius of the present age." However, Mao was the only

Communist leader allied with the Soviets to not attend the funeral; Zhou Enlai went instead.

On June 25, 1950, world attention again turned to war, this time in Korea. The 450-mile long Asian peninsula shares its northern border with China and a tip of Russia. The country was annexed by Japan in 1910, and at the end of World War II, the United States and the Soviet Union divided the nation temporarily along the 38th parallel. North Korea came under the sphere of the Russians and South Korea was adminis-tered by the Americans. In 1949, both U.S. and Soviet forces withdrew.

North Korea, with Soviet support, built a huge army, and in 1950 crossed the 38th parallel into South Korean territory. The United Nations Security Council called for a cease-fire and withdrawal of North Korean troops. North Korea ignored the order. In response, the United States sent troops to aid South Korea, and the Korean War began.

China was still recovering from World War II and the Communist takeover, and Mao did not want to be involved in another war at this point. But neither did he want a capital-ist Korean state and an American military presence looking over his shoulder. He told Stalin that China's entry into the war would be a defensive move. If the United States occupied all of Korea, he said, the next step would be war with China. So, Mao called for Soviet help before ordering in his army. The Soviets agreed.

Mao sent his troops to aid North Korea in late October, expecting full-scale Soviet air cover. However, Stalin was fearful of a possible nuclear challenge from the United States, so Soviet aid was limited. Even so, the Chinese entry into the war made victory impossible for the U.N. troops. In January

1951, Chinese and North Korean armies launched a massive attack across the 38th parallel and captured the South Korean capitol of Seoul. U.N. forces took it back in March. The fighting went on.

Early in the Korean War, Mao suffered a personal tragedy when his oldest son, Anying, age twenty-eight, was killed. The young man, one of Mao's sons with his late wife Yang, had returned from the Soviet Union to be reunited with his father. Anying volunteered for service, but for his safety was assigned to headquarters as an interpreter. It was no good though: an incendiary bomb hit the building where he was working in November 1950.

Anying was buried where he died. When Mao was told of his son's death, he agreed that the body should remain in Korea as an example to the Chinese people. Mao said in a

Mao with his son, Anying, in 1949 *(Courtesy of Gamma/Eyedea/ZUMA Press)*

brief public announcement: "In war there must be sacrifice. Without sacrifice there will be no victory. There are no parents in the world who do not treasure their children."

By June 1951, it seemed clear that victory in the Korean War was impossible for either side, so the countries agreed to peace talks. Agreement was reached a year later. After all the fighting, the war really settled nothing. A demilitarized zone (called the DMZ) was created between the Koreas. It cuts across the peninsula, 155-miles long and 2.5-miles wide. The DMZ remains the most heavily fortified border in the world.

Both North and South Korea were left in ruins. More than 2 million troops from the north were killed, about half of them Chinese. South Korea lost more than 100,000, including 33,000 Americans. However, China and Mao emerged stronger than ever, despite the cost of the war in money and life. Once again, Mao had shown the valor of Chinese fighting forces. They had fought the U.S. army, and brought it to a standstill.

The Korean War changed Mao's feelings toward Stalin. The Chinese had come to the Soviets' aid by preventing the collapse of North Korea. But it was Chinese troops, not Russian, who had fought the decisive battles. Mao would take no more orders from Stalin and the Soviet Union.

Even during the war, Mao focused attention on reforms. After the war, these efforts intensified. They were well received in the wake of anti-American sentiment that flooded China. Marchers carried banners through Beijing showing U.S. President Harry Truman with bloody hands reaching out for China, and the people grew violently indignant at the atrocities supposedly committed by U.S. soldiers in Korea.

If they did not grow indignant, they were suspected of being anti-government. And that was not a good thing to be in Communist China.

In this explosive atmosphere, it was easy for Mao and the CCP to consolidate their power through any means—often by executing anyone they suspected opposed them. Within a space of six months, some 700,000 people with even the slightest links, real or imagined, to the Nationalists were executed or driven to suicide. About 1 million more were sent to suddenly established reform-through-labor camps.

Increasingly, Chinese society became regimented. The press was controlled by the government, and public religious practices were restricted.

In late 1951, Mao and other leaders launched the Three-Anti campaign, against corruption, waste, and bureaucratism (a term which Mao defined as laziness and inefficiency, not strictly bureaucracy). This was followed by the Five-Anti campaign, against fraud, tax evasion, bribery, embezzlement, and leaking state secrets. The Chinese people were encouraged to keep tabs on their neighbors. Thus, China became a nation of informers: neighbor spied on neighbor, children spied on parents, brother against brother, all for the good of the state. In this manner, it is estimated that the anti campaigns resulted in the loss of several hundred thousand lives, mostly by suicide.

Mao's administration also set out to reform China's agriculture. About 30 percent of China's arable land belonged to a small group of landlords. Production was only 75 percent of what it had been in 1936. Mao instituted the Agrarian Reform Law, eliminating the centuries-old landlord class and putting the land in the control of the peasants. They did not actually own land, but they farmed in collective units, pooling materials, labor, and tools.

The average farming collective had about 170 families. Each family shared the work and production, but lived separately. Each family was also allowed a small plot of land to grow vegetables or livestock. Some free enterprise remained, but the farm system was now largely socialist.

The transition to collective farming was somewhat successful, but bloody and tumultuous. Many peasants took out years of frustration against the landlords, assaulting the former landowners. It is estimated that more than 1 million landowners died.

Like in the Soviet Union, high-ranking members of the Communist party became the rulers of the China. They were the leaders in schools, industry, the military, and in the villages. Each citizen belonged to a party-controlled unit, which determined where and how one lived, where vacations were spent, and sometimes even one's marriage partner.

In spite of the Korean War, the staggering task of rebuilding the country, and the deplorable methods that were used, Mao succeeded in this early transition to socialism. By the end of 1952, he had restored China's agricultural and industrial production to prewar levels. Crime, prostitution, and the killing of infants were almost unheard of. Westerners had departed, leaving their wealth and property behind. Now all Mao had to do was rebuild China into the ideal Communist state.

In 1954, delegates attended the First National People's Congress, which is China's national legislature. The state constitution was adopted, and Mao Zedong was elected chairman (or president) of the People's Republic of China. Zhou Enlai became premier of the new State Council.

Delegates at the First National People's Congress in 1954. Mao stands in the middle of the front row. *(Courtesy of AP Images)*

Even before he was named chairman, Mao had begun implementing his changes on Chinese society. From 1953 to 1957, Mao began enacting what is known as the First Five-Year Plan. It was set up to boost Chinese industry and start the country on the path to becoming a world-class power. Led by Mao, Zhou Enlai, and other revolutionary figures, it was modeled on the Soviet economic plan. Its basis was state ownership, large collective units in agriculture, and centralized economic planning.

Soviet engineers and technicians helped develop and install industrial facilities. Financial pressure induced private firm owners to sell them to the state or go into joint private-public companies that were state owned. By 1956, more than 67 percent of all modern industrial Chinese companies were state owned. State factories and mines were given a quota to meet for the year. Failure to do so was regarded as failing the Chinese people and taken quite seriously.

Farmers were encouraged to organize larger and larger collective units. This happened in steps. At the lower stage, the amount of income to each family depended on how much land each contributed to the cooperative. In advanced coop-

Crude iron smelters being tended by Chinese workers in 1959. It was around this time that heavy industry in China began expanding. *(Courtesy of AP Images)*

Mao (second from left) visiting farm workers to congratulate them on production figures in 1958. *(Courtesy of Keystone/Hulton Archive/Getty Images)*

eratives, money was paid on how much labor was contributed. By 1957, more than 93 percent of Chinese farm households were part of advanced cooperatives.

By most standards, the First Five-Year Plan was quite successful. Heavy industry expanded; iron and steel manufacturing, coal mining, and electricity plants were modernized. However, although agriculture output increased, the leaders were concerned that state companies were unable to increase the amount of grain needed in the cities. A run of bad seasons coupled with the confusion of transferring to the new system discouraged many of the peasants about Soviet-style farming.

After Stalin died in 1953, Nikita Khrushchev became head of the Soviet Union. For some time, Mao had realized that the Soviet style of government was not necessarily ideal for China in all aspects. And when Khrushchev began to criticize Stalin and his authoritarian bureaucracy, Mao's beliefs were affirmed. Wanting to avoid the unrest that occasionally showed up in the Soviet Union, Mao decided to encourage more people, especially intellectuals, to take part in government and even criticize the party. In a speech in May 1956, he said: "Let a Hundred Flowers Bloom, Let All the Schools of Thought Contend." He encouraged people to voice their thoughts just as long as those thoughts were constructive and not hateful. He also noted that leaders were often misunderstood, just as Jesus and Confucius had been.

It was a curious speech, but it did—slowly at first—bring on criticisms. Almost every intellectual—scientists, artists, and writers among them—had something to complain about. Once freed to speak, intellectuals increased their attacks

Mao (right) speaking with Nikita Khrushchev, who became head of the Soviet Union in 1953. *(Courtesy of AFP/Getty Images)*

on the CCP. In addition, students began to riot and workers demanded better wages.

But Mao began getting nervous about radical changes in the Communist world. A revolt in Hungary in November needed the Soviet military to prevent overthrow of the Communist government. Mao saw the revolt as the result of a more liberal government in Hungary over the past few years, and he and other party members grew increasingly afraid that a similar revolt might occur in China.

Mao decided it was time to end the "Hundred Flowers" movement. On June 8, 1957, an editorial in the *People's Daily* noted that criticizing the government was no longer encouraged. In another editorial, Mao claimed that the Hundred Flowers campaign was actually a success, but had unfortunately been undermined by a small group of extremists who did not want China to progress. Later, Mao republished his earlier "On the Correct Handling of the Contradictions Among the People" speech. In it he talked of poisonous weeds and fragrant flowers. He made it quite clear that the weeds were those who criticized the party. From then on, the weeds were arrested, brainwashed, sent out to work in the fields, or silenced in other ways.

Indeed, even before the Hundred Flowers movement officially ended, Mao began suggesting that the whole campaign had been a ploy to trick those who would criticize the government to publicly reveal themselves, making it easier for the CCP to weed them out. Mao launched the Anti-Rightist campaign to quickly eliminate those whose criticisms Mao deemed as hateful or disloyal. The purges that he ordered included members of the CCP. Those suspected of not being totally committed to the party line were condemned as rightists, such as the ministers of forestry and communications, who Mao claimed were anti-Communist. By the end of 1957, about 300,000 people were labeled as rightists and therefore against the government.

Most of the rightists purged by Mao were intellectuals. Many of those who weren't killed or imprisoned lost their faith in Mao and CCP. Though the dissidents had been routed out, Mao and the Chinese government had lost many of the very people needed to build a new and strong nation.

six

The Great Leap Forward

*M*ao was determined to industrialize China, to create a modern socialist society from a land of largely illiterate, semifeudal, peasant farmers. He was also determined to do it quickly. This was an astonishingly ambitious project. What had taken the Soviets four decades to accomplish, Mao said China could do in one. He envisioned a nation that in a short period would match both Soviet and American industrial output.

It became clear by late 1957 that the First Five-Year Plan was not a rousing success. In fact, during the previous year, the first phase of collective farming resulted in widespread famine. So, in January 1958 an enthusiastic Mao Zedong unveiled an ambitious second five-year plan, to run from 1958 to 1963. It was known as the Great Leap Forward.

The central idea of the Great Leap was that agriculture and industry would develop not only rapidly, but at the same time.

This involved almost unbelievable physical efforts by Chinese workers. Basic to its success was the people's commune. The first experimental commune was set up at Chayashan in Henan in April 1958. Communal kitchens—where everyone ate together much like in the military—were introduced for the first time.

After that, almost the entire Chinese population was rapidly organized into communes. Each commune was a self-governing, self-sufficient group of 5,000, 10,000, or more families, much larger than the old collectives. Within the commune, people ate, slept, and worked as one huge

Mao delivering a speech in 1957 *(Courtesy of AFP/Getty Images)*

family. In the countryside, about 26,000 communes replaced the more than 700,000 farm collectives. Urban communes were not successful. Work points were given in the communes instead of wages and money. These places were not merely agricultural settings; they also contained light industry and construction projects.

Quemoy and Matsu

In the midst of China's economic problems in 1958, Mao decided to attack two offshore islands, Quemoy and Matsu. They were controlled by Chiang's government in Taiwan. He believed that the United States would not go to war over such tiny pieces of land. Mao hoped that his attack on Taiwan would force the Nationalists to leave the island and surrender.

Mao guessed wrong. President Dwight D. Eisenhower decided to back Chiang by sending the U.S. Seventh Fleet as protection for Nationalist ships that were supplying the two islands. An international controversy was averted when Mao and the Communists, in the face of the U.S. threat, backed down.

Commune households were organized into a military-type lifestyle. The peasant families ate in mess halls. Each family donated its farm animals and tools to the commune as well as most of its personal property such as furniture. Side by side, men and women worked long hours with few breaks in the day. In fact, women were encouraged to leave their household chores and join the work force, known as brigades. The brigades worked from dawn to dusk tilling the fields and constructing irrigation and water conservation projects.

Before the Great Leap Forward, individual family plots of land accounted for about 30 percent of the peasants' income and about 7 percent of the country's crop cultivation. After one year of the Great Leap, there were no family plots of land. Everything belonged to the commune.

The commune controlled every aspect of people's lives: distributing food, organizing the work day, filling production quotas, and sending what was required to the government.

Perhaps such a gigantic, ambitious plan was doomed to failure no matter what the effort. However, the Great Leap Forward was not helped by Mao's almost blind faith in peasant power and his distrust of intellectuals. Having already killed or brainwashed many of China's educated with the Anti-Rightist movement, there were few strong minds left for Mao to turn to, and he rarely asked the few that remained for expert opinions, often with disastrous results. An example is what happened with steel production.

In August 1958, the decision was made to double steel production within a year. After seeing a backyard steel furnace in operation, Mao ordered one built in every city neighborhood and every commune. The idea was to make steel out of scrap metal. The production quotas were wildly optimistic. To meet them, the furnaces were fed with practically anything that would burn: workers' furniture, pots and pans, water buckets, rakes, hammers, nails, hinges, and barbed wire. And, of course, fuel was needed for the smelting pots; entire forests were cut down to keep the fires burning. Workers were pulled off the farms and factories and put on steel production.

A backyard steel furnace in operation during the Great Leap Forward. *(Courtesy of Jacquet-Francillon/AFP/Getty Images)*

But Mao had not spoken to any experts on the best methods for producing steel, and no one who realized that Mao was barreling forward without considering numerous facts and contingencies was going to criticize the chairman's plan. The result was that the backyard steel furnaces produced low-quality steel that was of little use anywhere. Mao visited a steel factory in Manchuria in early 1959 and learned that only reliable fuel such as coal could make quality steel. The backyard steel furnace program was quietly shut down later in the year. It left behind acres of hillsides scarred by erosion because the trees were gone; they were not replaced for some thirty years. Even worse, the fact that so many workers had been taken from producing food to making steel would soon become an even bigger problem.

Similar difficulties cropped up in construction projects, where experts were often not consulted. Radical ideas in agriculture also failed. Even so, at the summer conference in 1959, few party leaders had anything critical to say about the Great Leap. The only one who dared to denounce it was Marshall Peng Dehuai. Mao promptly fired him as defense minister.

Party leaders might not have said much at the summer meeting, but by then the peasants were grumbling. The Great Leap Forward was not embraced by the people. They disliked eating in mess halls; when they had food, they ate by themselves. Where they could, the peasants began once again to plant their own crops, tired of putting all of their efforts into serving the state.

In addition, the management of the communes was not going as well as Mao forecast. Commune leaders were more likely to have their positions because of patriotism rather than skill or experience. As a result, in order to look good, they often inflated crop production figures when reporting to the government. The government used the inflated figures to make the next year's production quotas even higher, which of course the communes could not meet.

Despite all the problems, the weather in 1958 promised a good harvest. But so many people had been pulled from the fields to work in steel production that much of the crop was left to rot. After the cities and other urban areas got their share, the peasant workers had little. In many areas, they starved, especially after a bad harvest in 1959, and the flooding of the Yellow River in East China.

By 1960, weather conditions were worse. Northern China experienced drought and the south was swept with typhoons, flooding out much agricultural land. More than 100 million acres of land was devastated by drought, and another 50 million ruined by floods. Before long, the peasants were too hungry and weak to continue their work to meet the government's unrealistic production quotas.

Between 1958 and 1962, it is estimated that 30 million or more Chinese died from starvation, mainly in the countryside. Perhaps 15 million fewer children were born. The exact figures, however, are not known.

The Chinese Communist Party (CCP) was unwilling to admit it made mistakes in the planning of the Great Leap Forward. Mao did not take any responsibility for the failure: in fact, to avoid any reference to failure or poor planning, the years between 1959 and 1962 were officially referred to as Three Years of Natural Disasters. Also, the party did not reveal to the Chinese people or the world the extent of the famine. This was partly to save face with the Russians. To

In this 1962 photo, Chinese refugees beg for food after escaping to Hong Kong. *(Courtesy of AFP/Getty Images)*

the millions who went hungry, an explanation was not going to feed them anyway.

During this period, Chinese relations with the Soviet Union were falling apart. Mao had initially welcomed Khrushchev's leadership, but became disenchanted after the Soviet leader began to distance the Soviet Union from the Stalin era. Meetings between the two grew troublesome.

In 1957, when Mao was in Moscow, Khrushchev proposed a secret agreement between the two countries. The Soviets would provide nuclear weapon technology; in return, Mao was to support Khrushchev and back Russia's number one position in the world Communist movement. Mao agreed. However, the following year Khrushchev proposed two jointly owned radio stations to keep in touch with the Soviet submarine fleet in the Pacific as well as a joint Soviet-Chinese nuclear submarine flotilla. In other words, the Soviets would build a navy for China but it would be maintained under their direction, a kind of co-op fleet.

To Mao, these plans were too much like the unequal treaties China had suffered from Western nations. To Khrushchev's chagrin, Mao refused the proposal.

One of the most talked-about meetings between Mao and Khrushchev is the 1958 swimming pool fiasco. When the Soviet leader was in Beijing, Mao called a meeting at his swimming pool. Khrushchev hated water and had never swum in his life. When he arrived, he was given a pair of baggy swim trunks and a life preserver. Then he was carefully led into the pool, where Mao was floating about like a rather bulky porpoise. Interpreters tried to conduct business with little success until Mao finally relented and moved the meeting to a wooden shed nearby. The course of Sino-Soviet relations went pretty much downhill from there.

The last time Khrushchev visited Beijing was in the late summer of 1959. He wanted Mao to release two imprisoned American pilots. As he had many times before, Mao refused

Khruschev's request. The following year Khrushchev called home all Soviet technical advisors in China, to the detriment of the Great Leap. Khrushchev also accused Mao of straying from a true Marxist doctrine.

Although he did not accept responsibility for the failure of the Great Leap, Mao decided to fade into the background in 1960. He was sixty-seven years old. He retained his supreme position as chairman of the party, but stepped down as head of state. He was replaced by Liu Shaoqui as chairman, Zhou Enlai as premier, and Deng Ziaoping as general secretary. To them, Mao left the task of digging China out from economic chaos.

Their response to the economic disaster was to retreat from commune economics and to focus more on individual effort. This displeased Mao but he went along with it. Industry remained state-owned, but skilled workers now received promotions and raises instead of slogans. Thousands of small, unprofitable factories were closed. The number of workers in industry was drastically cut, with many going back to the farms where it was felt they would be more productive.

The size of the communes was reduced, and each was given more freedom to set its own quotas. Untrained managers were replaced with trained party members. The commune school system was abolished and declared a failure. However, the party attempted to keep the mess halls as well as the order against private plots of land. This time, the peasants refused to accept these rules. The party, not wishing to make an issue of it, gave in. About 12 percent of China's arable land was given back to private ownership and production.

The harvest was good in 1962. With that incentive and to encourage the efforts of the peasants, Zhou Enlai made an announcement for the government and the party. He declared that China's economic recovery was complete.

seven

Witch Hunt or Quest for Culture?

A s Liu Shaoqi, Zhou Enlai, and Deng Ziaoping set to work repairing China's economy and scaling back the Communist reforms Mao had introduced, the chairman grew uneasy about what he saw as emerging capitalist, anti-socialist tendencies. The party seemed to be shunting him aside, turning him into nothing more than a figurehead. The material incentives offered to the peasants for better work were, to Mao, corrupting and counterrevolutionary.

Mao Zedong could no longer stay in the wings as his country changed direction. And so in 1963, at the age of seventy, he began to reappear in public, such as being photographed swimming in the Yangtze River. He openly attacked Liu Shaoqi, and he criticized the government policies that had moved China away from Communists ideals he had fought for.

A meeting of top Chinese Communist leaders in 1962. From left: Zhou Enlai, Chen Yun, Liu Shaoqi, Mao, and Deng Ziaoping. *(Courtesy of AFP/ Getty Images)*

To halt a trend toward capitalism, Mao launched the Socialist Education Movement, a drive to sharpen political consciousness in the villages. It was aimed primarily at schoolchildren. Although it had little immediate effect on politics, it did leave a mark on a generation of young Chinese. The movement called for cleanup in four areas: politics, economics, ideas, and organization.

Political purity must be restored, said Mao. Revolutionary fervor must be brought back to the party and the government.

Mao (front) swimming in the Yangtze River *(Courtesy of AP Images)*

The class struggle must be taken up again. Mao called on all Chinese to learn from the struggles of China's People's Liberation Army (PLA). With the support of his wife Jiang Qing, minister of defense Lin Biao, and Chen Boda, a leading theoretician, Mao systematically gained control of the party by mid-1965.

Mao greatly feared that the revolution he had fought for might not survive his death. Therefore, he hoped to create a social and political structure in China that would forever define the nation. In 1966, he introduced the Great Proletarian Cultural Revolution. Whether or not it permanently defined China, it did bring in a decade of deliberate upheaval. Beginning as a struggle for power within the Chinese Communist Party, it expanded to include large segments of society and eventually brought the country to near civil war.

Perhaps fittingly, the Cultural Revolution began with a play. Called *Hai Rui Dismissed from Office,* it concerned an honest official who is fired by a corrupt emperor. The author was Wu Han, deputy mayor of Beijing. The play was a thinly disguised reference to Mao's dismissal of Peng Dehuai after the Great Leap failure. In 1965, Mao's wife, Jiang Qing, wrote an article in a Shanghai newspaper that criticized the play, even though Mao had at first praised it. The article said the play was an attack on Mao and called it a poisonous weed.

Jiang Qing's article got a lot of publicity, and other newspapers picked it up. This caused Beijing mayor Peng Zhen to protest that the criticism had gone too far. He set up a committee called the Group of Five. On February 12, 1966, it issued a report, later known as the February Outline. The report said that the fuss over the play was academic, not political. In response, Jiang Qing published more articles, this time criticizing both Wu Han and Peng Zhen.

On May 16, the Cultural Revolution began when the Politburo issued a document called Notification from the Central Committee of the Communist Party of China. Mao personally revised the document seven times before presenting it to the public. The Notification discredited the February Outline, and called for the disbanding of the Group of Five. It branded Peng Zhen and his allies as traitors, turning their backs on Communism in favor of ushering capitalism into

China. A year later, the *People's Daily* ran an editorial calling the Notification a great historical document and praising comrade Mao for his great leadership—it was the first official document of Mao's Cultural Revolution.

Later in the year, a new Cultural Revolution Group (CRG) was formed, headed by Chen Boda. Jiang Qing and Zhang Chunqiao were made his deputies. Peng and others were to be investigated for anti-party conduct. In speech after speech, the CRG extolled the genius of Chairman Mao, beginning what came to be known as the "Mao cult of personality."

In 1964, the first publication of what is best known as "The Little Red Book" appeared. Compiled by Lin Biao, *Quotations from Chairman Mao* contained excerpts from Mao's speeches and writings and covered every aspect of Communist doctrine. It quickly became the bible of the Cultural Revolution. Slogans, quotes, and mottos sprang from it like a mantra. There was no problem that could not be solved, no evil that could not be cleansed by reading *Quotations from Chairman Mao*.

By unleashing the Cultural Revolution, Mao intended to rid the country of all threats to his authority. To do so, he deliberately led China through a violent, prolonged period of death and destruction. According to Mao, there must be a mass movement to purge China of the old ways that threatened the revolution. Old thoughts, old customs, old habits, and old culture must be eliminated. Nothing in China's long history was sacred.

Mao found a diverse group of allies in his drive to cleanse the land. One was defense minister Lin, who not only published "The Little Red Book" but ordered every soldier in the PLA to read it. He also changed the uniform of the PLA, getting rid of all insignia and signs of Soviet-style officer status. This simpler approach was more in keeping with Mao's guerrilla-type warfare in earlier years. Under Lin's direction, the PLA was praised as a great atmosphere for the training of revolutionary leaders and fighters.

Another ally was Mao's wife, Jiang Qing, who had stayed out of politics for years. But after a trip to the Soviet Union in 1956, she formed a group of those interested in culture

Quotes from Mao's "Little Red Book"

An army without culture is a dull-witted army, and a dull-witted army cannot defeat the enemy.

Political power comes out of the barrel of a gun.

There is a serious tendency toward capitalism among the well-to-do peasants.

We shall heal our wounds, collect our dead and continue fighting.

Women hold up half the sky.

Imperialism is a paper tiger.

Politics is war without bloodshed while war is politics with bloodshed.

War can only be abolished through war, and in order to get rid of the gun it is necessary to take up the gun.

The people, and the people alone, are the motive force in the making of world history.

To read too many books is harmful.

Lin Biao in 1971 reading from the "Little Red Book" (*Courtesy of AFP/Getty Images*)

and the theater. She believed that revolutionary attitudes must be part of the cultural world. As a result, with Mao's backing, Qing became the judge of Chinese culture, deciding if works passed the test of socialist values. All forms of artistic expression in China were soon subject to severe and stifling censorship, as artists struggled to create works that met the impossible socialist standards of the government. Even a group of leftist intellectuals supported the Cultural Revolution. While they had previously been stifled in their criticism of the government, Mao's Cultural Revolution created an environment that allowed these intellectuals and activists to speak out, so long as they spoke out in support of Mao and Communism.

To imprint his enduring legacy upon China, Mao chose young people as his main instrument. Judge your elders, he urged China's youth. Destroy the old thoughts and habits that are destroying the revolution. Middle-school teenagers, responding with the enthusiasm of the young, were joined by students in the universities to demonstrate for the cause. They came to be known as the Red Guards, defenders of Mao, backers of the revolution, readers of "The Little Red Book."

On June 1, 1966, an editorial in the *People's Daily* said that all those who were linked to imperialists—meaning anti-revolutionists—had to be eliminated. A month later, Red Guard representatives wrote to Mao saying that so-called mass purges were justified.

Even Mao could not have been prepared for what followed. Youthful enthusiasm developed into brutal fanaticism. Teenaged squads of Red Guards ran through the towns and villages, assaulting—and often killing—anyone they regarded as representing China's past. In this manner, libraries, temples,

A group of Chinese children stand in front of a picture of Mao while reading Mao's "Little Red Book" in 1968. *(Courtesy of Hulton Archive/Getty Images)*

museums, and universities were smashed and destroyed, all in the name of the new, the revolution.

On August 8, 1966, the Central Committee passed the Decision Concerning the Great Proletarian Cultural Revolution. Also known as the Sixteen Points, detailing the freedoms granted in the People's Republic, it made clear that the country was undergoing a great revolution to purge the land of anything or anyone that so much as criticized the road to socialism. All loyal Chinese were expected to crush those who strayed from this objective.

With this document, the Red Guards suddenly gained status. It was suddenly their duty to join the nationwide campaign to save their country, an authorized mission. Thousands of young people, some as young as nine, left their schools and their jobs to join the Red Guards. They could spout Mao's quotations by heart. They were pro-revolution and anti-everything else.

But quickly their fervor again turned into chaos and violence. In addition to killing or destroying anything they

The Sixteen Points

The freedoms granted in the document of August 1966 later became part of the People's Republic constitution. They are listed as four great rights in a great democracy: to speak freely, to be heard, to write posters, and to hold debates. The document also added the right to strike, but when the country was in massive civil disorder in 1967, the army severely limited that right. In 1979, after Mao's death, all these rights were deleted from the constitution.

believed in conflict with Mao's Cultural Revolution, the massive gangs of Red Guards were so disorganized that they began fighting amongst themselves. The result was massive civil disorder. In the violence and chaos of this period, it is estimated that perhaps half a million people died and millions were persecuted. Blame fell on Mao, and his encouragement of this destruction in the name of his revolution.

On August 16, 1966, Mao and Lin Biao spoke in Tiananmen Square in Beijing. Some 11 million Red Guards gathered there to see their leaders and be praised. All during

Red Guards marching in 1966 *(Courtesy of AP Images)*

that autumn, Mao reviewed gigantic parades in the square. Thousands of Red Guards marched by, waving "The Little Red Book" and chanting his quotations. A short time later, Mao issued a public notice that stopped police from interfering in any actions by the Red Guards. Anyone who tried to stop the beatings or killings or the destruction would be branded a counterrevolutionary. In September, another notice urged all Red Guards to visit Beijing, fees paid for by the government.

For about two years, the Red Guards continued their rampage under the watchful but benevolent eyes of Mao and the party. They even expanded their efforts to reconstruct the country along socialist lines. One method was to pass out leaflets giving the names of supposed counterrevolutionaries. They held public meetings to criticize people and wrote plays to educate the public. Activists for the cause became so violent that some began to steal weapons from the army. Up to that point, the party leaders had encouraged all actions of the Red Guards. Now, even Mao began to worry about what he had started.

Counterrevolutionaries were not the Red Guards only targets. They also hated the Soviet Union, backing Mao in pulling away from the Soviet bloc. They demonstrated against the United States, its involvement in Vietnam, and its capitalist ideology.

In the wake of all the destruction caused by the Red Guards, what was left of the ransacked temples and monasteries became warehouses. Buddhist monks were led off to manual labor. In the cities, a kind of mass hysteria developed as everyone tried to prove their loyalty. Politicians denounced their rivals. Officials in various government offices were often thrown out of their workplaces and their files destroyed. Leaders who were thought to be less than enthusiastic about the cause might be dragged into the street and forced to march with dunce caps on their heads. Many judged to be evil or disloyal were simply beaten to death. Many, knowing what was coming, committed suicide.

In the paranoia of the time, a power struggle developed among central government officials. Everyone accused everyone else of wrongdoing. Mao's wife was behind the so-called January Storm in 1967 when city leaders in Shanghai were criticized and removed from their jobs for disloyalty. Through another editorial in the *People's Daily,* Mao praised all the infighting. He said that all government leaders—national and local—should criticize themselves and others. This erupted into constant power struggles as official after official tried to demonstrate loyalty by purging someone else. It seemed the only safe way to keep one's job. In some cases, local governments stopped working altogether.

In July, the Red Guards were directed by Qing to take over for the People's Liberation Army if needed. Increasingly, the Red Guards stole from army barracks and looted military buildings, and the army proved powerless to stop them.

By late 1967, Mao finally decided the violence must end. The chaos was even too much for him. By this time, Liu Shaoqui, Deng Ziaoping, and others whom Mao regarded as shifting to capitalism were purged from public life. Their families were humiliated. Liu was expelled from the party forever, went to a detention camp, and died there in 1969. Deng underwent re-education therapy a number of times and was sent to work in an engine factory. Some years later he was re-instated by Zhou Enlai. Most of those in government who were accused of being disloyal suffered worse fates: some were tormented for years, accused of various crimes; some were never heard from again. Children of parents or grandparents who were suspect often tried to clear their own names by destroying their relatives' homes, family photographs, or works of art.

Mao ordered the PLA to stop the Red Guards. Lin Biao, who was now promoted to Mao's chosen successor, told the Red Guards to stop fighting and study the works of Mao. But no one paid any attention, and the chaos and deaths continued. Mao, seeing that the violence he had helped set in motion would not be easily stopped, ordered the Red Guards to be broken up. They had failed in their mission, he declared.

The Red Guards were officially dismantled in July 1968. Many of them were confused by their sudden drop from power and esteem. Many fought back, until the government sent in large units to subdue them. A number of Red Guards were sent to labor camps for their disobedience.

Mao felt that what was left of the Red Guards would be less troublesome in the country. So, he ordered the Down to the Countryside Movement, which lasted for about a decade. Recently graduated middle-school students were ordered to go to the countryside. They were finally allowed to return to their cities in the late 1970s.

The Red Guards had done their work; Mao no longer needed them. From now on, he would rely solely on the PLA to maintain order. He directed the army to form revolutionary committees in all the provinces.

Today, most people inside and out of China regard the Cultural Revolution as a disaster. No one in power officially defends it. The Chinese Communist Party's official position is that the Cultural Revolution occurred because party and state institutions were destroyed. That can happen, says the party, when one person builds a cult of personality. To prevent another cultural revolution, China's leaders rely on a strong party structure where decisions are made collectively and are not in the hands of one individual.

eight

The Last Years

I n April 1969, the Ninth National Party Congress con-
firmed Mao Zedong as the supreme leader and signaled
the end of the Cultural Revolution. Some historians,
however, say this was only the end of the activist phase and
that the revolution continued for nearly a decade.

However long it continued, Mao's Cultural Revolution
affected nearly every Chinese citizen. At its end, the rail-
way system was in shambles, and the educational structure had come to a halt. China's museums were devastated:
thousands of years of history were almost totally destroyed
in a few short years by the violent fervor of the Red Guard.
Minority groups suffered greatly. Books of the Koran were
destroyed. Ethnic Korean areas in northeast China were
wiped out. The human rights of millions of Chinese were

erased. Mao had started this, and now he was faced with a nation to rebuild.

With some 60 percent of former party leaders purged, Mao was ready to start his rebuilding first with the Chinese Communist Party (CCP). Two-thirds of those at the Ninth Congress were in the military, indicating Lin Biao's growing importance as Mao's successor. New party members were now limited to those with humble—presumably meaning peasant—backgrounds.

As Mao's second in command, Lin was known for his brilliant army record; he never lost a battle. His rise in the Communist ranks was slow, however, in part perhaps due to poor health. In 1958, he was named to the seven-person Standing Committee of the Politburo. The following year he became defense minister. His publication of Chairman Mao's thoughts in "The Little Red Book" aided his unexpected jump into second place in the government. Lin also played a prominent role in directing the army throughout the Cultural Revolution. His favored status was solidified in 1969 when the new constitution referred to Lin as "Mao Zedong's closest comrade in arms and successor."

But relations between the two men soon began to sour. They disagreed on agricultural policies and on the continuing role of the army. Mao began to see the economy in slightly more liberal terms, whereas Lin wanted to hold on to methods used in the Cultural Revolution. Lin was against any closer ties with the Soviet Union or the United States, whereas Mao was at least considering such moves as being in China's interest.

In addition, Lin continuously requested promotions within the party and central government. This made Mao suspicious:

he feared that Lin might want to take over while Mao was still alive. In turn, Mao's suspicions put Lin in a difficult position, and he knew it. Lin had said of Mao: "Once he thinks someone is his enemy he won't stop until the victim is put to death; once you offend him he'll persist to the end—passing all the blame on to the victim, held responsible for crimes committed by himself."

What happened next is somewhat of a mystery. Officially, the government says that Lin feared Mao had turned against him. Therefore, Lin planned an assassination plot. Others say that Mao decided to reduce Lin's power by planning a purge. Lin learned of it and plotted a military coup in late 1970. This is known as Project 571, a play on Chinese monosyllables to mean armed uprising. Supposedly, Mao (whose code name was B52) was supposed to die when his private train blew up on returning from an inspection tour of southern China. Lin's plan involved his wife, his son Lin Liguo, and some military supporters. But some say the plot was strictly the work of Lin Liguo and that Lin knew nothing about it.

According to the official report, Lin's daughter exposed her father's plot against Mao. If that part is true, it is in keeping with the times since children were encouraged to spy on their parents for the good of the revolution.

There were apparently some assassination attempts against Mao in 1971 in Shanghai. Some of the reports were conflicting and some proved to be outright false. However, after September 1971, Lin never again appeared in public. Many of his military backers fled to Hong Kong, and about twenty army generals were arrested.

On September 13, 1971, Lin and his family reportedly attempted to flee the country via jet to the Soviet Union.

That night, their plane mysteriously crashed in Mongolia, several hundred miles from the Sino-Soviet border. All were killed. Stories circulated for a long time after the crash. Some said the plane was shot down by Soviet or Chinese forces. Whatever the truth, the rancor between Mao and Lin suggested that China's new leaders were hardly different from those they had so long sought to defeat: at the bottom of all their struggles was the determination to hold personal power at all cost.

Meanwhile, Mao's personal life was mired in turmoil as well. In the same way that Mao had lost interest in his second and third wives, he now showed little regard for his fourth wife, Jiang Qing, with whom he had one daughter, Li Na. Believing that sexual activity leads to long life, Mao engaged in affairs with dozens of young women. Qing knew of the affairs, but had no power to stop them. And while Mao had frowned on and discouraged the Chinese people from attending dance parties, operas, movies, and other activities he deemed bourgeois and decadent, he bent the rules to satisfy his own pleasures, at times watching banned foreign films on an almost nightly basis.

In other ways, Mao's personal habits remained relatively unchanged from the days of his peasant upbringing. He never combed his hair, brushed his teeth, or bathed. Instead, his bodyguards wiped his body, hands, and face with hot towels, and cut his hair. To freshen up his mouth, Mao rinsed with tea in the morning and then ate the tea leaves. As a result of not brushing, a green patina coated his teeth, but it did not bother Mao, who reasoned, "a tiger never brushes his teeth."

Expensive clothes never appealed to Mao, either; he often conducted business in worn robes, patched pajamas, and slippers. Even when he made a public appearance, which was rare, he wore a plain gray tunic buttoned to the neck.

As power struggles against "enemies" within the Chinese Community Party continued to dog Mao, his conduct reflected a growing paranoia. Nonetheless, he continued to push his policies, holding meetings with senior party leaders at all hours of the day and night, and usually from his large, specially made bed or while lounging by an indoor pool at the Chinese leadership compound.

Following the death of Josef Stalin, Mao had moved continuously away from the guiding influence of the U.S.S.R. For a time, the split between the two countries was kept relatively quiet. China felt the Soviets were appeasing the Western countries. But both the Soviet Union and the United States

Russia Backs Down Over Cuba

The Cuban Missile Crisis began on October 16, 1962, during the so-called Cold War between the United States and the Soviet Union. U.S. reconnaissance planes showed that Soviet nuclear weaponry was being installed on the island of Cuba, ninety miles off the U.S. coast. The missiles were supposedly placed there to protect the island from an American attack. The Soviets likened them to U.S. nuclear warheads in Great Britain, Italy, and Turkey.

U.S. President John F. Kennedy warned Soviet premier Nikita Khrushchev that unless the missiles were removed, there would be war. Twelve days later, on October 16, Khrushchev announced the dismantling of the missiles. Most experts say this was the closest the two countries ever came to nuclear war.

by now had massive nuclear capability, and neither wanted war. In addition, Khrushchev was not about to deliver nuclear weapons to a China that was in an upheaval over domestic problems.

The split became public in mid-1960 when, at the congress of the Romanian Communist Party, the two countries openly criticized each other. Heated words continued until the final rupture in 1962. Mao spoke harshly against Khrushchev for backing down during the Cuban Missile Crisis. At the same time, the Soviets openly supported India during its brief war with China. The fight was over a shared Himalayan border. China declared a ceasefire after it captured the disputed areas.

Khrushchev fell from power in October 1964, replaced by Leonid Brezhnev and Alexei Kosygin. Zhou Enlai went to see them but reported no change in the Soviet position. During the Cultural Revolution, there was no contact between the two countries. Diplomatic relations were never broken but were decidedly frozen. Red Guards at one point in the madness attacked the Soviet Embassy in Beijing. As civil war threatened China, Mao backed down on confrontations with the Soviets. However, in 1969, armed clashes broke out between Chinese and Soviet troops along the border. By this time, China had detonated its first nuclear device, although it could not compare with the Soviet arsenal. By 1970, many experts were predicting war between the two Communist giants.

At this point, Mao considered his situation. He faced massive internal disorder. He could not cope with that and fight the Soviet Union or deal with a possible U.S. confrontation. And so he called the United States.

While Sino-Soviet relations had been worsening, a slight thaw was growing with the West, thanks largely to the diplomacy of Zhou Enlai. Mao thought that China might use the United States as a buffer against the Soviet Union. Political advisor and later secretary of state Henry Kissinger was asked to Beijing in secret in July 1971. He and Zhou laid the groundwork for U.S. President Richard Nixon to visit China.

U.S. President Richard Nixon visiting Mao in 1972 *(Courtesy of National Archives)*

Nixon's visit took place in February 1972. It was the first time a U.S. president had visited China, and was integral in building diplomatic relations between the two countries.

Nixon spent a week in China, meeting Mao and Zhou Enlai numerous times. The two governments signed the Shanghai Communiqué, a statement that promised to work toward full diplomatic relations. Though there was controversy over the U.S.'s diplomatic relations with Taiwan—China claimed that the country was still a part of China, and therefore not a country to be recognized by the U.S.—the meeting with the Americans was a success for Mao.

After Lin Biao's death, it was suddenly unclear who would succeed Mao, who was seventy-seven years old. Two factions developed, each trying to set themselves up to take control in the inevitable and fast approaching occasion of Mao's death. One side was made of longtime CCP party members, led by Zhou Enlai and Deng Ziaoping. They were opposed by a group of radicals who came to power and influence during the Cultural Revolution. This group was led by Jiang Qing, Mao's wife (who dreamed of becoming premiere herself), Zhang Chunqiao, Yao Wenyuan, and Wang Hongwen; the Gang of Four as they came to be called.

During the last years of Mao's life, a power struggle developed between the Gang of Four and the senior party members. The Gang started a campaign to weaken the authority of premiere Zhou Enlai. Mao himself feared that Zhou had gained in power from the ashes of the Cultural Revolution. But perhaps by this time the Chinese people had grown weary of the constant purges against government members. At any rate, this campaign got nowhere and was dropped.

In October 1975, Zhou became gravely ill and was hospitalized. Deng was named first vice premier and continued Zhou's work on modernizing China. The following January, Zhou died of bladder cancer. At his official funeral, attended by great crowds in the square in Beijing and across the country, Deng delivered the official eulogy.

It did not take long for the Gang of Four to seize this opportunity. The only major politician opposing them was Deng Ziaoping, so they started a campaign against him, apparently with Mao's approval. However, when it came time to name a new premier after Zhou's death, Mao did not select one of the Gang of Four. Instead, he chose the relatively unknown Hua Guofeng.

The fifty-five-year-old, chubby faced Hua—his detractors called him "pumpkin head"—was a Hunan politician of no particular talent. He was, however, doglike in his devotion to the chairman. Despite his advancing age, Mao wanted to continue to hold onto his power, and because he distrusted both Deng and the Gang of Four, the fiercely loyal Hua was a shrewd choice. In April 1976, Hua was officially appointed premier of the State Council.

On April 5, crowds gathered in Tiananmen Square for a traditional day of mourning called the Qing Ming Festival. Although they were officially mourning the death of Zhou Enlai, they also expressed hatred toward the Gang of Four. Posters against the Gang appeared and threats were shouted. Some 2 million people gathered in and around the square, turning the mourning festival into a heated protest against the Gang's activities.

The Gang of Four, in response, called in the police to disperse the crowds. In addition, they blamed Deng Xiaoping

Mao chose Hua Guofeng to be the new premier of China after Zhou's death in 1976. *(Courtesy of AP Images)*

as the inciter. Officially, this protest and response are known as the Qing Ming Tiananmen Square incident (not to be confused with the Tiananmen Massacre when the government stopped student protests in 1989.)

Meanwhile, Mao's health was taking significant turn for the worse, as it had been for many years. Mao suffered from various ailments in his later years. He had respiratory problems from years of smoking. In 1974, he was blind for a time until cataract surgery the following year. Other serious health problems were diagnosed. One report said Mao had amyotrophic lateral sclerosis (ALS), better known as Lou Gehrig's disease, which causes total destruction of the muscles. Another report said he suffered from Parkinson's Disease, a degenerative disorder of the nervous system causes shaking and muscle rigidity

Mao reportedly suffered two heart attacks in May and June of 1976. His mind remained alert, so the Politburo members held some of their meetings in the swimming pool area near his rooms. But on September 2, a third attack, more serious than the others, sent him into a coma. He recovered enough to read some reports on September 8, but again drifted into a coma that evening. Politburo members surrounded his bedside when he died shortly after midnight on September 9, 1976.

It was a stunning moment for the CCP and the nation of China. Mao had been the leader of China for the most of the twentieth century: millions of Chinese citizens had never known a world without Chairman Mao. Now Mao was dead, and the future of China was uncertain.

As Mao was buried in Tiananmen Square, flags of the People's Republic of China were displayed at half mast and

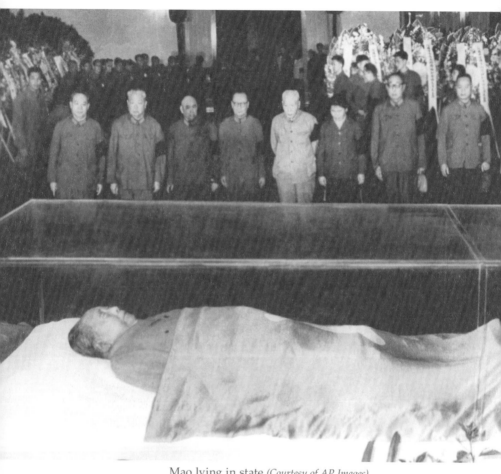

Mao lying in state *(Courtesy of AP Images)*

a week of mourning was ordered. Some 300,000 people filed past his casket during that week. Tributes came in from all over the world. The UN flag in New York City flew at half mast. That was more honor than displayed in Russia, which acknowledged his death in the newspaper *Izvestia* with two lines on a back page. Taiwan responded to the news with celebrations around the island.

At the end of the official mourning week, a million people

stood in the Square of the Gate of Heavenly Peace in Beijing. At three in the afternoon, work was stopped all over the country and sirens blared. By four o'clock, it was back to work as usual, and a new era for China had begun.

The World's Largest Public Square

Mao Zedong is buried in Tiananmen Square, the largest public square in the world. It is about as long as nine football fields, encompasses ninety-three acres, and can hold more than 500,000 people—which it sometimes has. The square, directly south of the Imperial Palace in the Forbidden City, is at the center of Beijing.

The square was not always so large. Chinese emperors did not want large groups of people to gather in one place. Mao started the renovation in 1949. Later renovations in 1976 and 1981 enlarged it to its present size. It is surrounded by government and national buildings

Tiananmen is the site of many demonstrations, such as the declaration of the People's Republic in 1949, Cultural Revolution rallies in 1966, the observation of Mao's death in 1976, and the student protest riots in 1989. Military parades are held there on every fifth-year anniversary of the founding of the People's Republic.

Tiananmen Square *(Courtesy of AP Images/Ng Han Guan)*

nine

The New China

O n October 6, 1976, shortly after Mao's death, Hua, elevated to position of chairman of the CCP, ordered the arrest of the Gang of Four and some of their lesser cohorts. All arrests were carried out without bloodshed. Then, a massive media campaign was launched deriding the Gang for their excesses during the Cultural Revolution. It is at this point that many say the Cultural Revolution really came to an end.

The Gang of Four went through a show trial in 1981. They were accused and convicted of activities against the party. Qing was the most defiant, although Zhang also declared his innocence of any charges. Yao and Wang confessed and repented.

At the trial, the court said that nearly 800,000 people had been persecuted. The true figures will probably never be known since many deaths went unreported or

Zhang Chunqiao (far left), Wang Hongwen (third from left), Yao Wenyuan (fourth from left), and Jiang Qing (center, with glasses), collectively known as the Gang of Four, stand trial in 1981. *(Courtesy of AFP/Getty Images)*

were covered up by police or the Guards. In addition, the People's Republic is not anxious to allow serious research into this period.

Qing and Zhang were given death sentences, later changed to life imprisonment. Wang got life and Yao was sentenced to twenty years. All of them were later released. According to reports, Qing committed suicide in 1991, Wang died in 1992, Zhang in April 2005, and Yao in December of that year.

Now relatively free to govern, Hua tried to reverse the damage of the Cultural Revolution. Even though he had ordered the arrest of the Gang of Four, he still backed Mao. His policy became known as the Two Whatevers. China should continue to obey whatever Mao said, declared Hua, and keep on with whatever Mao decided.

Hua intended to return China's political and economic system to the Soviet style. But pressure from the central committee forced him to restore Deng to state affairs. Deng was named vice premier of the State Council and at the Party's Eleventh Congress, he was ranked behind Hua as a member of the Politburo Standing Committee.

But number two was not what Deng wanted. Through the newspapers in 1978, he began to attack Hua's policies, especially ridiculing the Two Whatevers. At the congress held that December, Deng called for thoughts to be liberated within the party and he again attacked Hua. At the congress in 1980, many of those purged during the Cultural Revolution were reinstated. Hua resigned and Zhao Ziyang was named the new premier. Deng became chairman of the Central Military Commission.

Deng had a strong influence on China during his years in government and until his death in 1997, although he never did gain the country's top leadership position. He is credited with China's modernization and dramatic economic improvement. He was the first Chinese leader to visit the United States, meeting with President Jimmy Carter in 1979.

Since Mao's death, China's leaders embarked on reforms that have encouraged peaceful cooperation and economic development. They have allowed more economic freedom, with privately owned companies leading the way. China is more open to foreign investment and trade. In 2007, Chinese construction firms were hard at work rebuilding a railroad in the African nation of Angola. Chinese engineers cleared the rapids on the Mekong River in northern Thailand, allowing Chinese-manufactured products to reach Southeast Asia.

Experts believe that the new leadership of China wants to take a larger role in world affairs. Much of the country's recent economic success is due to the efforts of Hu Jintao, China's leader since 2003. He is president of the country,

Deng Ziaoping meeting with U.S. President Jimmy Carter. Deng is credited with improving the economy and modernizing China after Mao's death. *(Courtesy of AP Images)*

chairman of the Central Military Commission, and general secretary of the CCP. He represents China's transition from old-time leaders like Mao to the younger technocrats. He is a tireless ambassador for China. However, there are no signs that China will change its political policies and outlook. Hu has been involved with the top levels of the Communist Party most of his life. Since he took over, he restored some controls on the economy and is considered conservative when it comes to political reforms.

Despite the surprising rate of economic growth, China remains a poor country with many internal problems. There is no pension system for workers. Its cities are polluted and environmental clean-up plans are nonexistent. Rural workers are constantly upset over conditions. They fire up protest demonstrations on a regular basis. One of the ways to measure a country's economy is the gross domestic product, or GDP. It is the market value of all goods and services that a country produces within a given period of time. In 2006, the GDP per person in China was $1,700, compared to $42,000 in the United States. It is estimated that China spends about

Hu Jintao, China's leader since 2003 *(Courtesy of AP Images/Greg Baker)*

1.55 percent of its GDP on the military; the United States spends 3.9 percent.

Many Chinese leaders feel that this is the century for their country to become one of the world's chief leaders. It is expanding trade with such areas as Southeast Asia and is conducting good relations with former enemies such as India. In 2005, for instance, the two countries signed a treaty in which China gave up any claim to the state of Sikkim.

Yet China is still what it was in Mao's time, a one-party state. It wants no interference in its own affairs by other countries. In return, China does not delve too closely into the affairs of other countries. China will make deals based on what will benefit its economy. As a result, it deals with democracies such as Australia as well as the government of Zimbabwe, noted for massive human rights violations. As do many nations, China uses its power as a permanent member of the U.N. Security Council to further its own interests. It diluted a U.N. resolution that tried to stop the ethnic slaughter in the Sudan. China owns 40 percent of an oil company in southern Sudan, and its growing economy needs the oil. However, the Chinese government does not widely involve its troops in U.N. missions; only about 1,400 are currently in peacekeeping missions worldwide.

Marxism-Leninism is alive and well in China. Its leaders will always follow the party line.

The modern leadership of China wants to concentrate on the future and has little to say about the past, which includes the leadership and policies of Mao Zedong. For instance, in 2006, the government did not even mention that it was the fortieth anniversary of the Cultural Revolution. That period, which officially ended with the fall of the Gang of Four, seems off limits for debate. There is no official memorial to the victims of that period.

The government's unwillingness to discuss these things is partly, experts say, because it is embarrassed by the scale of brutality and violence. Few young people in China today know the true story. Too close a look into the past might inflame long-held but suppressed animosity toward the government.

The official party stance is that Mao Zedong was a great leader who made a few mistakes. That may be the official party line, but Mao is still worshipped today by many Chinese, not as a living hero but as a dead god. His rural village of Shaoshan is a popular tourist spot. The house where Mao was born is preserved. A twenty-foot silver statue of Mao stands

A large statue of Mao in his hometown of Shaoshan *(Courtesy of AP Images/Chien-min Chung)*

outside a museum dedicated to him in Shaoshan. Inside, there are no indications that the Great Leap Forward or the Cultural Revolution ever occurred. The schoolhouse where he studied in Changsha is adorned by a fifty-foot-high portrait of Mao in the center of the auditorium. Many of the visitors are young, those who do not know about the persecutions. The cult of Mao lives on.

Some Chinese regard Mao as a great revolutionary leader, even while they acknowledge his mistakes. Even those who disagree about him as a leader do agree that he was a brilliant political and military strategist.

Three Kingdoms

Three Kingdoms, the historical novel that Mao read during his childhood, remains popular, except nowadays children around the world have the option of buying a video game version of the book. Eleven editions of the Playstation game currently exist, and more are sure to come. "Players will need to dig deep within to prove themselves adept at both military and political arts in order to bring China under one rule," a description on the game's packaging says. "More than 40 base commands give players the power to govern cities, manage their personnel, practice diplomacy, and much more."

Comic book versions of *Three Kingdoms* are available today, too. Near the end of one, a warrior laments the futility of trying to change fate and the course of history. "My Lord, you are set to bring the chaos to an end," he says. "This is your benevolent intention, but since ancient times chaos and order have come and gone unpredictably. . . . One can neither ignore one's fate nor can one fight against it." Many will agree that the fictional warrior's statements are all too true.

Mao supporters point to the fact that he unified China and brought in the greatest social reform in history. He created a peasant movement that carried him and the CCP to power. They credit him with China's social and economic development. At his death, illiteracy was less than 7 percent and life expectancy rose from thirty-five to more than seventy years.

Mao also influenced many Communist governments around the world, such as the revolutionary movement in Nepal and the Communist Party of Peru. He became an inspiration for anti-colonial movements worldwide. Many of them include Maoism in their doctrines, as does the Revolutionary Communist Party, USA. However, since his death China has moved sharply away from Maoism.

Many historians consider Mao one of the twentieth century's most brutal dictators, on a par with Hitler and Stalin. He is responsible for the deaths of perhaps more than 70 million people. In addition to the brutality, Mao's detractors point to his failings in establishing the rosy society he promised. Socialism would bring a new culture to China. But writers and teachers were prevented from the personal expression that establishes and defines a culture. And the people who were to benefit from this new culture became those who learned from experience that it was not a good thing to think individually or outside the established socialist box.

Mao is certainly held responsible for the disasters he inflicted on China with the Great Leap and the Cultural Revolution. Millions of victims died as a result. But it cannot be denied that, whatever the methods or consequences, he totally changed his country.

Mao Zedong

Mao's legacy may ultimately rest with how well and distinctly he is remembered by his people. Therefore, it may be noteworthy that in 2006, the Chinese government issued a new set of history textbooks for high schools in Shanghai. Socialism now merits a single chapter. Communism in China before 1979 is covered in one sentence. There is very little about the French or Bolshevik revolutions, but there is a lesson on neckties. The government says it wants people to think more about the future of China than its past.

In the new texts, there is no section on Mao, except for one mention in a chapter on etiquette. The life and the lessons of Mao Zedong are now only taught to junior high school students in Shanghai, China.

Timeline

1893	Born December 26 in Shaoshan Village, Hunan province.
1908	Forced by father, Rensheng, to marry cousin; wife dies in 1910.
1911	Joins a local army unit and plays minor role in revolution that deposes the ruling Manchus.
1919	Starts job as librarian in Beijing; marries Yang Kaihui, daughter of his former professor.
1921	Co-founds the Chinese Communist Party (CCP).
1927-1928	Marries third wife, He Zizhen; organizes and leads Autumn Harvest Uprising against Chiang Kai-shek's forces; campaign fails.
1930-1931	Nationalists capture second wife, Yang, and oldest son, Anying; Yang executed; establishes the Chinese Soviet Republic in Jiangxi Province.
1934	Leads the Long March of the Red Army from Jiangxi Province to Yenan; hundreds of thousands die, but the army escapes defeat by Nationalist forces.
1937-1945	Second Sino-Japanese War breaks out; leads

resistance against Japanese Occupation; elected chairman of the CCP Central Committee, a position he will hold until his death.

1949   Communists defeat Nationalist armies and force Chiang to flee to Taiwan; retains chairmanship of CCP; declares People's Republic of China (PRC); takes first trip abroad to Moscow.

1950   Backs North Korea in invasion of South Korea; fails due to U.S. intervention.

1951-
1952   Sanctions mass trials against counter-revolutionaries—intellectuals, artists, writers, professionals, foreigners, Christian missionaries; 1 to 3 million executed.

1953   Introduces first five-year plan.

1954   Elected chairman (president) of the People's Republic.

1957   Makes second trip to Moscow.

1958   Launches The Great Leap Forward.

1959   An estimated 16 to 30 million people starve due to famine caused by Great Leap disaster; replaced by Liu Shaoqi as president.

1962   Breaks with Soviet Union; China-India border war.